EVALUATING
QUALITATIVE
RESEARCH

JEASIK CHO

EVALUATING QUALITATIVE RESEARCH

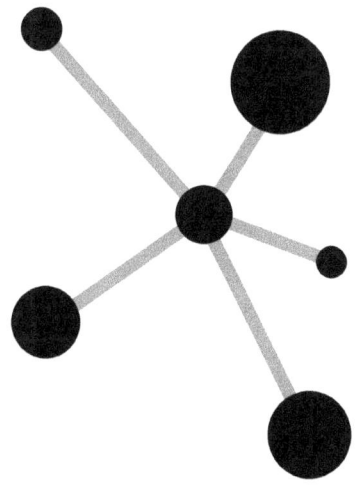

OXFORD
UNIVERSITY PRESS

OXFORD
UNIVERSITY PRESS

Oxford University Press is a department of the University of Oxford. It furthers
the University's objective of excellence in research, scholarship, and education
by publishing worldwide. Oxford is a registered trade mark of Oxford University
Press in the UK and certain other countries.

Published in the United States of America by Oxford University Press
198 Madison Avenue, New York, NY 10016, United States of America.

© Oxford University Press 2018

CIP data is on file at the Library of Congress
ISBN 978-0-19-933001-0

CONTENTS

CONTENTS

PREFACE

This book was written to provide the qualitative research community with some insight on how to evaluate the quality of qualitative research. To my knowledge, this topic has gained little attention during the past few decades. It appears that we, qualitative researchers, do in fact know about this topic and participate in evaluating the quality of qualitative research in our everyday lives. We read journal articles, serve on masters' and doctoral committees, and also make decisions on whether conference proposals, manuscripts, or large-scale grant proposals should be accepted or rejected. As such, we do these kinds of intellectual and practical jobs, formally and informally. Some may say that one could do these jobs primarily based on Lincoln and Guba's (1985) and Guba and Lincoln's (1989) hallmarks of trustworthiness and authenticity. Others, such as Lincoln and Guba, may say that one could do these jobs by creating a different set of evaluative criteria embedded in one's own paradigms. Still others may say that one can do these jobs by simply applying intuition and/or personal criteria to a paper being reviewed.

These three explanations likely represent how we largely think about evaluating the quality of qualitative research. Nonetheless, until now, no textbook has been specifically devoted to exploring theories, practices, and reflections associated with the evaluation of qualitative research. Of course, there are many scholarly journal articles that demonstrate ways of judging the quality of qualitative research. Several books are also available that attempt to conceptualize how to evaluate the goodness of qualitative research from philosophical and scholarly standpoints. In effect, this book addresses these existing ideas and suggestions in accordance with a typology of evaluating qualitative research that I have constructed. To further advance this topic, this book has collected information from websites and qualitative journal editors and reveals ways in which manuscripts on qualitatively studies are evaluated. Last, this book illustrates some challenges that are currently encountered by the qualitative research community with regard to the set of evaluative criteria that constantly evolve, debates on politics of evidence, and the fast growth of mixed methods research.

The following is a remark on the evaluation of research from a popularly known introductory research text (Creswell, 2008):

> The audience for your report will have its own standards for judging the quality and utilities of the research. Evaluating research involves assessing the quality of a study using standards advanced by individuals in education. Unfortunately, there are no ironclad standards for evaluating educational research in the academic research community. (p. 286)

Readers are invited to join me in confidently rewriting this quotation as follows: "Fortunately, there are commonly agreed, bold standards for evaluating the goodness of qualitative research in the academic research community. These standards are a part of what is generally called 'scientific research.'" The next generation had better be informed of the spirit of qualitative research in this way in their first research textbooks. It is my hope that this book will contribute to the fulfillment of this wish.

ACKNOWLEDGMENTS

This book would not have come to light without Dr. Patricia Leavy's consistent support. Her amazing insights into the proposal of this book and her caring mentorship throughout the past few years are beyond my description. Thank you from the bottom of my heart. As always, I am also thankful to my eternal mentors, Dr. Robert Donmoyer, Dr. Patti Lather, Dr. Laurel Richardson, Dr. Grechen Rossman, Dr. Norman Denzin, Dr. Francisco Rios, Dr. Paul Klohr, Dr. William Pinar, Dr. Won Hee Lee, Dr. Ho Sung Choi, and Dr. Young Chun Kim, for being my professional role models during the past several decades. Your lofty research and scholarship on qualitative research and education have always provided the food for my intellectual growth. I am indebted to many wonderful qualitative journal editors who shared ideas and information on this topic with me. Thank you for your kindness and support. I am grateful to my friends, Dr. Angela Jaime, Dr. Kevin Roxas, Dr. Suk Min Choi, Dr. Peter Moran, Dr. Joan James, Dr. Cindy Brock, Dr. K "Tao" Han, and Dr. Sang Han Kim, who have walked with me even on rainy days. In addition, a special thanks to Mr. David Henry, who has taught me how to become a better human being through tennis. Steven, Peggy, Dick, and Martha's unconditional love always reside in my heart. Many thanks to Dr. Patricia McClurg and Dr. Michael Day for your continuous support. Last, I thank my lovely wife, You Su, and two wonderful children, Sky and Lucia, for always encouraging me and giving me happiness.

EVALUATING
QUALITATIVE
RESEARCH

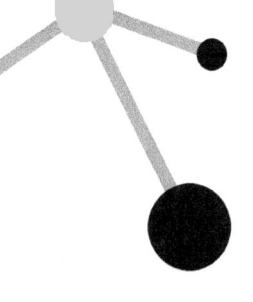

GETTING INTO THE FIELD

Quality is elusive, hard to specify, but we often feel we know it when we see it. In this respect research is like art rather than science.

—Seale (2002, p. 102)

Many proposal writers make the mistake of talking about validity only in general, theoretical terms, presenting abstract strategies such as bracketing, member checks, and triangulation that will supposedly protect their studies from invalidity . . . magical charms that are intended to drive away evil; they lack any evidence for how these strategies will work in practice, and their use seems to be based largely on faith in their supernatural powers.

—Maxwell (1996, p. 88)

THE PURPOSE of this book is to explore ways of evaluating the processes and products of qualitative research. During the past few decades, the discourse on the evaluation of qualitative research has been scattered. The theories and practices of ethnographic and qualitative methods from the 1970s to the present are well known. In addition, much is known about the "paradigm war" between the qualitative and the quantitative camps; the proliferation of different qualitative research paradigms; and the innovative/culturally relevant, reflexive turns under what is generally called postmodernism (Denzin & Lincoln, 1994, 2000, 2005, 2011). Nonetheless, there are several ongoing issues regarding the evaluation of qualitative research, including (1) the fact that there is little agreement on the nature of evaluation in qualitative research, (2) the continuous impact of traditional positivist evaluation criteria on qualitative research, and (3) the broad political discourse on the politics of evidence.

During the past three decades, there have been few studies on the proper ways of evaluating qualitative research. Although a few seminal ideas and instruments for assessing qualities of qualitative research have been available, they have either remained the same or have made little progress (Ambert, Adler, Adler, & Detzner, 1995; Burns, 1989; Duncan & Harrop, 2006; Elliott, Fischer, & Rennie, 1999; Forchuk & Roberts, 1993; Greenhalgh, 1997; Guba, 1990; Guba & Lincoln, 1989; Inui & Frankel, 1991; Lincoln & Guba, 1985; Marshall, 1990; Morse, 1991; Smith, 1990). The book, *The Quality of Qualitative Research*, by Seale, was published in 1999 with an emphasis on clarifying the nature of quality from a particular philosophical standpoint—that is, a subtle realist approach, grounded in the intellectual tradition of the United Kingdom. Here, Seale is against the use of both traditional and constructivist approaches when judging the quality of qualitative research. His argument is that the traditional approach is too rigid to evaluate the complexity of the goodness of qualitative research, whereas the alternative approach goes nowhere, no matter which direction it takes. In the end, Seale proposes that the goodness of qualitative research can be judged by the extent to which a set of analytical and rigorous evaluation criteria are utilized. Similarly, Thomas Schwandt (2002), in his seminal book *Evaluation Practice Reconsidered*, deconstructs the ideas and practices of a traditional evaluation model that is less concerned with the values and beliefs of those under investigation, and then he establishes an alternative framework useful for taking the complexity of social practices into account. His viewpoint of this alternative evaluation framework falls into interpretivism or hermeneutics that value the multiplicity of social practices.

I agree with Schwandt's (2002) viewpoint that constructing an evaluation lens that involves general and specific accounts of what one might hope to find in a good study is exciting intellectual work. Schwandt's four general approaches to evaluating qualitative research include the use of universal conventional criteria, alternative criteria of trustworthiness and authenticity, pragmatic criteria, and subtle realist criteria of validity and relevance. Although I am impressed with his scheme for a developmental perspective on the evaluation of qualitative research, I believe that this kind of framework, by itself, is something like creating another repetition of what has already been deemed disagreeable in this field.

In 1994, Miles and Huberman, two pioneers of qualitative data analysis, wrote that "social phenomena exist not only in the mind but also in the objective world—and that some lawful and reasonable stable relationships are to be found among them" (p. 4). It is obvious that their approach to qualitative research is post-positivist in that reality can be in part discovered as is. In particular, rigor is greatly valued. A systematic inquiry process is believed to lead one to a truthful conclusion. With these strong assumptions (being objective, lawful, reasonable, or truthful) in mind, these two post-positivist researchers address an issue relative to the quality of conclusion. The following is a reconstruction of what is written in the section titled "Standards for the Quality of Conclusion" (p. 277). I ask Miles and Huberman about goodness criteria, imaginatively:

JEASIK: How do you know whether the finally emerging findings are *good*?

MILES: That term, *good*, has many possible definitions: (1) possibly or probably true, (2) reliable, (3) valid, (4) dependable, (5) reasonable, (6) confirmable, (7) credible, (8) useful, (9) compelling, (10) significant, or (11) empowering.

JEASIK: Is it enough to say that well-carried-out tactics will make *good* conclusions?

HUBERMAN: Yes and no! We can only explore some practical standards that could help us all judge the quality of conclusions. The battles in this domain have been extensive, and they continue.

JEASIK: Many interpretivist researchers suggest that it is really impossible to specify criteria for good qualitative work. I kind of agree with this position.

MILES: Qualitative studies take place in a real social world. There is a reasonable view of "what happened" in any particular situation. We who render accounts of it can do so well or poorly. We should not consider our work unjudgeable. In other words, shared standards are worth striving for.

JEASIK: So, your goodness criteria such as "possibly or probably true, reliable, valid, dependable, reasonable, confirmable, credible, useful, compelling, significant, or empowering" are those that are commonly used in the evaluation of qualitative research. What a list!

The aforementioned three key books associated with the evaluation of qualitative research make claims on evaluating the goodness of qualitative research by adopting a "neither–nor" approach (Seale, 1999), an "alternative" philosophical approach (Schwandt, 2002), or "a checklist" approach (Miles & Huberman, 1994). At this point, some readers may wonder why Lincoln and Guba's (1985) trustworthy criteria have not yet been discussed. This is because many contemporary scholars view Lincoln and Guba's goodness criteria as the alternative to evaluating qualitative research. I eventually deal with their criteria, of course. Please bear in mind that their criteria have been constantly revisited, criticized, and reconstructed. At this point, I simply argue that the evaluation of qualitative research has been long overdue for the global qualitative research community not only to look back at what has been accomplished but also to look forward with an expectation of how to do a better job for the external and internal stakeholders and users. Qualitative inquiry involves many different epistemological ideas and practical procedures. Newer theories and methods, along with advancements in technology, have constantly emerged (Leavy, 2014). Furthermore, under the circumstance of changing political climates, a difficult question needs to be asked regarding how one can be more savvy in constructing and thus advocating a holistic evaluation of qualitative research in which the parts and the whole are interconnected organically, conceptually, practically, and politically. What follows is a brief outline of what I make sense of the evaluation of qualitative research.

My initial feelings about the evaluation of qualitative research were similar to those of two outstanding scholars of grounded theory, Juliet Corbin and Anselm Strauss (2008). Both expressed their feelings regarding the evaluation of qualitative research: "[We] . . . feel paralyzed, unsure of where to begin, or what to write. [We] find that evaluation is necessary but there is little consensus about what that evaluation should consist of" (p. 297). Evaluation is indeed necessary by all means, and two entities—evaluation and research—may loosely coexist for decades. Qualitative research appears to be understood in most cases in comparison with quantitative research. Although such a comparative understanding is useful, larger discourses about qualitative research are likely to be paradigmatic or theoretical in nature. The necessity of having these discourses is obvious, but for this reason, there has been little consensus about what evaluation should look like.

What is evaluation? Evaluation is a judgment of one placing a certain value on something. Evaluation typically involves quality, which is abstract. Unlike quantity, quality can be differently understood by different people. The following are definitions of quality, standard, and excellence in the *Oxford Dictionary*.

> *Quality*: "the standard of something as measured against other things of a similar kind" or "the degree of excellence of something"
> *Standard*: "a level of quality or something used as a measure, norm, or model in comparative evaluations"
> *Excellence*: "the quality of being outstanding or extremely good"

It appears that the meanings of these words are interwoven with evaluation. To know a notion of quality, one needs to know other constructs, such as standard or excellence. However, a close look at the definition of quality reveals two indicators: *comparative standard* and *the highest degree*. The quality as a standard offers comparative evaluation, whereas the quality as an excellence indicates being outstanding or extremely good. To be certain, evaluation is a human act. Thus, concern with the quality as a standard/excellence falls into another layer of human judgment. Humans set up a level of standards against which quality is judged. Humans create a notion of being outstanding or extremely good. Quality, standard, and excellence are lenses with which one can assign certain judgments.

Then why is it so difficult to start "evaluating" qualitative research? Two simple but important reasons follow. First, Patton (2002) notes that

> some of the confusion that people have in assessing qualitative research stems from thinking it represents a uniform

perspective, especially in contrast to quantitative research. This makes it hard for them to make sense of the competing approaches within qualitative inquiry. (p. 543)

Second, Riessman (2008), a well-known scholar in narrative inquiry, warns,

In my reading of the debates, they turn on a set of questions about evidence and ethics. I prefer not to think in terms of standards or criteria, and warn students away from the "paradigm warfare" that exists in the literature. It can paralyze and, in my view, simplify what are complex validation and ethical issues all investigators face. (p. 185)

Seeing qualitative research from a uniform perspective in contrast to quantitative research is problematic, mainly because it is highly likely that a user will rely, intentionally or unintentionally, on conventional validity and reliability. This misled perception results from taking for granted the narrow definition of "what research is" from natural science. On the one hand, Riessman's (2008) caution about getting involved in the "paradigm warfare" that exists in literature is double-edged. Ignoring the paradigm warfare appears to ignore an important historical development of qualitative research with regard to a justification of method. However, it is equally truthful that once investigators get involved in the paradigm warfare, it is dangerous to simplify complex validation and ethical issues.

Two major evaluative concepts are important to mention here. One is a broad meaning of evaluation practiced qualitatively, and the other is the well-known trustworthy criteria. Not only do both concepts serve as a foundational understanding of the evaluation of qualitative research but also they help lead us to move forward. First, according to Greene (2000),

Evaluators do not just claim to know about something, they claim to know how good it is from selected vantage points. . . . [E]valuators rarely practice a "pure" form of their craft, either philosophically or methodologically. The complex, pluralistic demands of evaluation field contexts evoke instead multiple, diverse frames of guiding practice and invite dialogue among them. In fact, evaluation expertise today is marked by its dialectical, dialogical temperament, its openness to multiple forms and layers of understanding, its responsiveness to contextual needs for understanding, rather than its adherence to any singular philosophy or approach. (pp. 983, 988, emphasis in original)

By making a typology of contemporary program evaluations, Greene (2000) notes that "evaluation practiced qualitatively . . . strives to reach pluralistic ideals while clearly acknowledging its partialities" (pp. 991–992). Consequently, she addresses the challenges of evaluation as storytelling in terms of four evaluative questions: "How good is this story?" "How good is this program?" "Are you just advocating for your own viewpoint?" and "Whose interests are being addressed?" (p. 991). These fundamental evaluative questions provide the qualitative research community with a critical reflection on data, representations, and ethics.

Second, Lincoln and Guba's (1985) alternative criteria for evaluating naturalistic inquiry follow. Importantly, this set of evaluative criteria has been mentioned as a starting point in almost all qualitative research articles and books (Thomas & Magilvy, 2011, pp. 152–154):

Credibility: The elements that allow others to recognize the experiences contained within the study through the interpretation of participants' experiences; checking for the representativeness of the data as a whole; member checking involving returning to the participants for ensuring that the interpretations of the researcher are by the participants as accurate representations of their experiences; peer debriefing; prolong engagement (internal validity)

Transferability: The ability to transfer research findings from one group to another; thick description used to provide the reader with detailed contextual information; transfer of understanding is believed to occur if both contexts are similar (external validity)

Dependability: When another researcher follows the decision trail used by the researcher; having peers participate in the analysis process (reliability)

Confirmability: Self-critical attitude on the part of the researcher about how one's own preconceptions affect the research (objectivity)

In addressing the traditional goals of criteria such as internal validity, external validity, reliability, and objectivity, Lincoln and Guba propose *credibility, transferability, dependability*, and *confirmability*, respectively. I believe that the current discourse on evaluating qualitative research would not be as advanced without Lincoln and Guba's alternative approach to judging qualitative research. This alternative framework is still greatly influencing the field of qualitative research. Lincoln and Guba's construction of *trustworthiness* criteria is referred to as parallel criteria to traditional ones (Scheurich, 1996). Guba and Lincoln's (1989) other seminal book, *Fourth Generation Evaluation*, provides an updated version of the evaluative paradigm (for more details, see Guba & Lincoln, 1989, pp. 233–251).

Overview of the Book

I conclude this introductory chapter by providing an overview of the book. In Chapter 2, I explore many different approaches to evaluating qualitative research that can be classified into five categories: a general evaluation category of qualitative research, a "subtle-realist" category developed by Hammersley and Atkinson (1995) and Seale (1999), a post-criteriology category, an art-based research category, and a post-validity category. In Chapter 3, I demonstrate ways in which evaluation tools are practically discussed in literature and are actually used in qualitative research journals. Chapter 4 identifies several evolving evaluative themes. I conclude the book with Chapter 5, which discusses the present and future of qualitative research evaluation by referring to major findings from previous chapters. It is hoped that readers will bring a great deal of confidence, curiosity, and critical thinking to this book from their own fields of study because this book is intended to provide them with a sense of confidence to give a clear direction of where the evaluation of qualitative research was, is, and will be. The evaluation of qualitative research will continue to grow as all qualitative researchers curiously wonder what a core knowledge base can and should be for establishing firm grounded rules, transparently and fairly, used in many evaluation and funding proposal review contexts. In the end, because the evaluation of qualitative research is inseparable from a series of research undertakings such as identifying paradigms, formulating design, conducting fieldwork, and being mindful of ethics, what is needed is critical thinking from readers who will properly apply ideas discussed in this book to their own fields. With confidence, curiosity, and critical thinking in mind, I hope that readers will view this book as an invitation, not a recipe, so that all family members of qualitative research can revisit and thus upgrade discourses on quality, standards, and validity during lunch with colleagues or in research classes, offices, committee meetings, journal article reviews, and funding proposal reviews. Collective critical thinking will continue to make "EQR 2.0" (the evaluation of qualitative research 2.0) possible by means of constant self-, peer-, and community-based evaluation practices.

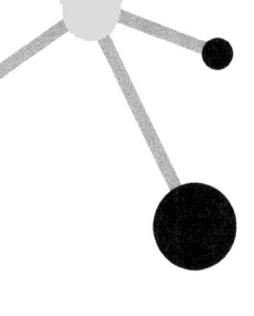

2

A TYPOLOGY OF THE EVALUATION OF QUALITATIVE RESEARCH

Toward a Holistic View

> Assessing qualitative research entails multiple and contradictory readings of its representational failures and successes. Therefore, validity of research is no longer conceived as a determination (i.e., "is valid" versus "is not valid") but a continual process of interrogation.
>
> —Aguinaldo (2004, p. 127)

THIS CHAPTER explores five specific categories of the evaluation of qualitative research (EQR) that have developed during the past three decades: (1) a general EQR category, (2) a "subtle realist" category developed by Hammersley and Atkinson (1995) and Seale (1999), (3) a post-criteriology category, (4) an art-based research category, and (5) a post-validity category. After briefly discussing these five categories, I share my holistic view of EQR by drawing a metaphor of a beehive. As noted in Chapter 1, EQR involves many kinds of considerations that include, but are not limited to, definitional, paradigmatic, political, and practical issues. For many, it has been regarded as a slippery, elusive concept that can be differently interpreted by different people. Therefore, it is hoped that EQR will be viewed from a holistic perspective, allowing evaluators from any field of study to choose necessary and sufficient ideas, criteria, or tools from these five categories of EQR.

A General EQR Category

Just like other fields of study, EQR is in need of a set of evaluative criteria that is broad enough to include a variety of qualitative research traditions. The question is, how broad is broad enough (Seale, 1999)? The field of qualitative research is broad in history, paradigms, theories, and practices. Each qualitative research tradition has its own rationale for quality considerations (Creswell, 2012; Denzin & Lincoln, 2011; Leavy, 2014). Although discipline-specific criteria for these research traditions are available, the majority of the literature on EQR attempts to provide general criteria or validity applicable to what is typically referred to as qualitative research (Box 2.1). Following the positivist research paradigm, these attempts have been published in many research articles during the past few decades, some of which are discussed in Chapter 3. Nevertheless, there is a dilemma with regard to these general attempts at EQR (Seale, 1999).

Here, I present a general EQR category that proposes evaluative guidelines intended to assist reviewers or committee members in making a judgment of the quality of any type of qualitative research. It may be viewed as too general for some types of qualitative research and perhaps too specific for others. This is a dilemma facing most qualitative research community members and outsiders as well (Seale, 1999). The following is an example of a general EQR category called the "10 Commandments for EQR": To my knowledge, almost every researcher/scholar/teacher has taken an introductory research class to learn how to conduct research. One commonly learns that research goes through a process similar to the following: problems → questions/purposes → literature review → context/setting → sample/participants → data collection/display/analysis/interpretation → significance of research. In addition, one learns about the human subject review process. Reviewing a research project in light of typical research procedures and components is common. Box 2.2 presents a review guideline used for the *Asian Journal of Educational Research and Synergy* that highlights a typical research process as *key evaluative criteria* (this journal accepts both quantitative and qualitative research).

Box 2.1. General Evaluative Criteria

How to evaluate dissertation studies or journal articles done qualitatively?

- Problem statement/research questions
- Research purpose
- Literature review
- Gain entry/research site
- Participants
- Data collection
- Data analysis/interpretation
- Validity/reliability/ethics
- Significance of the study

Last, *The Qualitative Research* journal (*TQR*) previously had an excellent preliminary review guide that described detailed evaluation procedures. Its point system follows:

> Every paper submitted to the journal receives a score and preliminary review. For those authors whose papers receive a score of 13 points or higher, their manuscript continues on through the *TQR* manuscript development process. For those papers receiving a score below 13 points, the authors are informed of their score and are given the opportunity to revise and resubmit their manuscript until a score of 13 points or better is achieved so the next steps of the manuscript development process can continue. (http://www.nova. edu/ssss/QR/Editorial/contrib.html)

> [Please note that TQR has since updated their policies, and the above is no longer available. However, the above link will show you different but useful information associated with their review process.]

Table 2.1 presents TQR's assessment rubric used in this preliminary screen (Chenail, Cooper, Patron, & TQR Associates, 2011). It consists of 10 performance areas: opening elements, introductory section, literature review, role of researcher, methods section, results section, discussion section, references, writing, and coherence.

Box 2.2. The *Asian Journal of Educational Research and Synergy's* Review Guide

General Considerations

1. Importance and interest to the journal's readers
   - What does the paper contribute to the field of education?
   - Is it significant to the target community?
   - Does it present a new and significant contribution to the literature?
   - Is it timely and relevant?
2. Originality of the paper
   - Is the study innovative? Interesting?
3. What was the author(s) trying to accomplish and was the author successful?

Specific Considerations

4. Presentation
   - Does the paper present a cohesive argument?
   - What is the basic logic of the presentation?
   - Are the ideas clearly presented?
5. Writing
   - Is the writing concise and easy to follow?
6. Length
   - What portions of the paper should be expanded? Removed? Condensed? Summarized? Combined?
7. Title
   - Is the title informative?
8. Abstract and introduction
   - Do the abstract and introduction accurately reflect the points made in the paper?
9. Literature review
   - Are the cited articles/papers current?
   - Is the literature review comprehensive?
   - Does the literature review contain a coherent argument supported by literature (as opposed to a list of studies)?
10. Methods for studies involving primary data collection
    - Does the author provide enough detail of the methodology?
    - Are the methods described clearly enough to facilitate replication (where applicable)?
    - Is there a sound research methodology?
    - Are the methods appropriate?

11. Data presentation
   - Could the design be conveyed more easily?
   - Are the data clearly presented?
   - Can the reported results be verified easily by reference to tables and/or figures?
   - Would another form of presentation help?
   - Are illustrations instructive?
   - Are all tables and figures clearly labeled? Necessary? Well-planned?
12. Analysis and interpretation
   - Does the organization of results promote understanding?
   - Are the analyses appropriate and logical? Are they described in enough detail?
13. Discussion
   - Are the discussion and conclusions made by the author supported by the data?
   - Does the writer understand the limitations of his or her work?
   - Is there enough breadth and depth in the implications of the study?

A "Subtle Realist" Category

This approach is pragmatic or post-positivist in nature. British scholars Hammersley and Atkinson (1995) and Seale (1999) make a strong case for the necessity of compromise between various extremes. Their philosophical stance in this regard is between idealism and realism, claiming that neither of them properly addresses a continuing tension of contemporary research, particularly in ethnography. Seale notes, "The widespread appeal of alternative conceptions of research is based upon some fundamental dissatisfactions with the scientific world view" (p. 7). Those who reside in this camp of thought believe that quality in qualitative research is "a somewhat elusive phenomenon that cannot be pre-specified by methodological rules" (p. 7). That is, those concerned with quality in qualitative research do not necessarily "give up on scientific aims as conventionally conceived, but also draw on the insights of post-scientific conceptions of social research" (p. x). For them, objectivism is viewed as "a resource that can be used productively as an attitude of mind by social researchers" (p. 25). Consequently, the discourse on EQR is not fixed but, rather, "open to the possibility that conclusions may

Table 2.1

The Qualitative Report's Preliminary Review Guide

Total Points out of 20 (Minimum 13 Points Required to Enter TQR Manuscript Development Program)

Author:

Title:

Performance Area and Criteria	Non-Performance: includes none or minimal important elements of performance area (0 points)	Partial: includes some but not all important elements of performance area (1 point)	Complete: includes all (or almost all) important elements of performance area (2 points)	Points:
1. Opening Elements: A. Title is 12 words or less B. Title indicates most important elements of report (i.e., population, focus, methodology, and findings) C. Abstract is 200 words or less D. Abstract reflects organizational structure of paper (i.e., presents problem/focus of study, research questions, participants, methodology, findings, and key points from discussion of findings) E. Paper includes Key Words F. Key Words include term for research method	Elements needing attention:	Elements needing attention:	All important elements included. –or– Only the following element is missing:	

	Elements needing attention:	Elements needing attention:	All important elements included. –or– Only the following element is missing:
2. Introductory Section: A. Statement of research problem B. Statement of research objectives C. Indication of why local study has global importance D. Statement of rationale for study E. Naming of intended audience F. Indication of benefit of research (answers the "so what?" question)			
3. Literature Review: A. Offers synopsis of current literature on topic in terms of content and research processes used B. Demonstrates gap in literature re: content and/or research methods C. Explains how study will fill gap D. Provides reflections on literature vs. series of reports on sources E. Includes literature that helps define phenomenon shows what is known and not known about phenomenon F. Explains how literature led to research questions	Elements needing attention:	Elements needing attention:	All important elements included. –or– Only the following element is missing:

(continued)

Table 2.1

Continued

Total Points out of 20 (Minimum 13 Points Required to Enter TQR Manuscript Development Program)

Author:

Title:

4. Role of Researcher:	Elements needing attention:	Elements needing attention:	All important elements included. –or– Only the following element is missing:
A. Describes researcher's context, interest in topic, and investment in study/intentions			
B. Makes clear who did what throughout study procedures			
C. Provides statement of IRB or other third-party approval secured to conduct study			
D. Describes how ethical issues were considered and addressed			
E. Describes how researcher bias was addressed			
F. Discusses steps taken to ensure rigor and trustworthiness of findings			
5. Methods Section:	Elements needing attention:	Elements needing attention:	All important elements included. –or– Only the following element is missing:
A. Explains how research design fits with research objectives			
B. Explains what type of qualitative inquiry was used			
C. Provides step-by-step description of procedures, with corresponding headings			
D. Describes sampling strategy and participant recruitment			
E. Explains steps of data generation, collection, and data analysis, as well as rationale for each design choice			
F. Cites literature used to guide procedures			
G. Tells reader what constitutes data			
H. Provides examples to illustrate steps of data analysis			

	Elements needing attention:	Elements needing attention:	All important elements included. –or– Only the following element is missing:
6. Results Section: A. Tells reader how results will be organized B. Tells reader how results are derived from analysis C. Findings produced consistent with methodology indicated D. Presents exemplary evidence to support findings E. Explains how each excerpt supports assertions/findings F. Each excerpt illustrates unique qualitative distinction (rather than including multiple quotes to illustrate one finding) G. Presents demographic information of participants in composite form			
7. Discussion Section: A. Does not include discussion in Results section B. Does not include findings in Discussion section C. Does not repeat information already presented in paper D. Discusses how findings compare/contrast with what was known and/or not known in the literature E. Discusses limitations of study F. Discusses position on generalizability of results G. Discusses implications of findings H. Indicates area of future research I. Ends paper with discussion section	Elements needing attention:	Elements needing attention:	All important elements included. –or– Only the following element is missing:
8. References: A. Citations in text correspond to sources in reference list B. References are in APA style	Elements needing attention:	Elements needing attention:	All important elements included. –or– Only the following element is missing:

(continued)

Table 2.1

Continued

Total Points out of 20 (Minimum 13 Points Required to Enter TQR Manuscript Development Program)

Author:	Title:		
9. **Writing**: A. Effective use of headings B. Fluent English language C. Clear, precise writing D. Correct grammar and usage E. Avoids bias in language F. Strong mechanics of style G. Active voice H. Contextualized language reflects interpretive stance	Elements needing attention:	Elements needing attention:	All important elements included. –or– Only the following element is missing:
10. **Coherence**: A. Between title and abstract B. Between abstract and body of paper C. Between focus of study and literature reviewed D. Between research questions and methodology E. Between methodology presented and methods employed F. Between methodology and findings G. Between findings and research questions H. Between findings and stated implications	Elements needing attention:	Elements needing attention:	All important elements included. –or– Only the following element is missing:

Source: Chenail, R. J., Duffy, M., St. George, S., & Wulff, D. (2011). Facilitating Coherence across Qualitative Research Papers. *The Qualitative Report, 16*(1), 263–275. Retrieved from http://nsuworks.nova.edu/tqr/vol16/iss1/17.

need to be revised in the light of new evidence" (p. x). A subtle realist category that is conceptualized in this pragmatic stance is convergent with the following point of view (Seale, 1999):

> Criteriology is, at root, an impossible project if it is intended to reflect an internally logical line of argument that simultaneously reconciles philosophical and political positions with the great variety of research practices which people may wish to pursue. The challenge appears to be to construct some general account of what we might hope to find in a good study that is, on the one hand, open enough to include this variety, and, on the other hand, not so loosely specified as to be no value in providing guidance. (p. 47)

The relationship between claim and evidence is a starting point for the subtle realist approach to EQR. Triangulating data in itself cannot warrant the credibility of a research report. Although it is useful to consider triangulation, subtle realists argue that "member validation offers a method for testing researcher's claims by gathering new evidence" (Seale, 1999, p. 71). The quality of qualitative research results from the degree of members' involvement. Openness to the possibility that conclusions may need to be revised in light of new evidence is determined by the extent to which members examine the closeness between evidence and claims.

Box 2.3 is an example of a review checklist by Seale (1999) from his seminal book about evaluating the quality of qualitative research. Seale organizes his major checklist items in terms of introduction (2 criteria), methods (5 criteria), analysis (6 criteria), presentation (6 criteria), and ethics (1 criterion), along with an additional 36 subcriteria following these major criteria.

To elaborate, under the Methods heading, Seale (1999) addresses typical issues related to procedures, such as the selection of subjects, theoretical sampling, the relationship between fieldworkers and subjects, and systematic ways of data collection and record-keeping. Under the heading of Analysis, he notes basic steps that should be followed: data analysis procedures (reliability); a degree of systematic analysis; adequate discussion of themes, concepts, and categories; negative case analysis; validity; and checking meaning with respondents. Last, under the Presentation heading is a synthesis of data that includes context specificity, a systematic data display, proper interpretation, an evidence-based

Box 2.3. A Review Checklist

....

Criteria for the Evaluation of Qualitative Research Papers

1. Are the methods of the research appropriate to the nature of the question being asked?
2. Is the connection to an existing body of knowledge or theory clear?

Methods

3. Are there clear accounts of the criteria used for the selection of subjects for study and of the data collection and analysis?
4. Is the selection of cases or participants theoretically justified?
5. Does the sensitivity of the methods match the needs of the research questions?
6. Has the relationship between fieldworkers and subjects been considered, and is there evidence that the research was presented and explained to its subjects?
7. Was the data collection and record-keeping systematic?

Analysis

8. Is reference made to accepted procedures for analysis?
9. How systematic is the analysis?
10. Is there adequate discussion of how themes, concepts, and categories were derived from the data?
11. Is there adequate discussion of the evidence both for and against the researcher's arguments?
12. Have measures been taken to test the validity of the findings?
13. Have any steps been taken to see whether the analysis would be comprehensible to the participants, if this is possible and relevant?

Presentation

14. Is the research clearly contextualized?
15. Are the data presented systematically?
16. Is a clear distinction made between the data and their interpretation?
17. Is sufficient original evidence presented to satisfy the reader of the relationship between the evidence and the conclusions?

18. Is the author's own position clearly stated?
19. Are the results credible and appropriate?

Ethics

20. Have ethical issues been adequately considered?

Source: Seale, C. (1999). The quality of qualitative research. London: Sage.

conclusion, the researcher's position, and credible results. Some of the subcriteria are as follows: Could a quantitative approach have addressed the issue better? To what extent are any definitions or agenda taken for granted, rather than being critically examined or left open? Has reliability been considered, ideally by independent repetition? Has the meaning of their accounts been explored with respondents? Are quotations, field notes, etc. identified in a way that enables the reader to judge the range of evidence used? and Have the consequences of the research been considered?

A Post-Criteriology Category

This category is seen as radical to some extent because those who reside in this category believe that it is neither desirable to have validity or criteria from the conventional positivist standpoint nor even possible to set up predetermined criteria for qualitative research that uncovers complex meaning-making processes:

> Is it possible to devise a set of goodness criteria that might apply to an inquiry regardless of the paradigm within which it was conducted? Or is it the case . . . that goodness criteria are themselves generated from and legitimated by the self-same assumptions that undergrid each inquiry paradigm, and hence are unique to each paradigm? (Guba, 1988, p. 16, as cited in Smith, 1990, p. 168)

Smith (1990) reviews three alternative paradigms and criteria—post-empiricism or post-positivism, constructivism, and critical theory—and finds an overall regulative ideal for inquiry—that is, "objectivity, solidarity, and emancipation" (p. 183), respectively. His criticism is focused on the assumption that "each paradigm has dispensed with the idea of an absolutely authoritative foundation for knowledge. This nonfoundationalism greatly complicates the criteria issue" (p. 183). There are at least three points similar to these different perspectives. First, there is no possibility that a mechanical decision-making procedure can be applied to distinguish valid from invalid research. Second, methodology or procedures, in and of themselves, are not sufficient for decisions about the quality of inquiry. Finally, although only briefly noted previously, none of the three perspectives has done very well in this area.

Regarding the matter of evaluation content and form, I have thus far presented a series of criteria, checklists, standards, and rubrics. I draw attention to another evaluation content and form that is different from that which was previously explained. If the previous strategies and discussions on determining the inclusion of evaluation criteria are straightforward and directive in terms of what qualitative research is like and how it proceeds, then the argument that Stiles (1999) makes is insightful and relational:

> The concept of objectivity is replaced by the concept of *permeability*, the capacity of understanding to be changed by encounters with observations. Investigators argue that we cannot view reality from outside of our own frame of reference. Investigator bias can be reframed as *impermeability*. . . . Good practice in reporting seeks to show readers how understanding has been changed. The traditional goal of truth statement is replaced by the goal of *understanding by people*. Thus, the validity of an interpretation is always in relation to some people, and criteria for assessing validity depend on who that person is (e.g., reader, investigator, research participant). (p. 99, emphasis in original)

To elaborate, according to Stiles (1999), EQR involves two sets of judgments on quality: *good practice criteria* and *validity criteria*. I briefly explain the first judgmental quality criteria. It is likely that all sorts of criteria mentioned in the previous content and form of evaluation thus far are convergent with what Stiles refers to as good practice criteria in light of the investigator's choice, sound analytical practices, and disclosures of the investigator's forestructure. The following are some example criteria: "Are research questions clearly stated? Are prolonged and persistent observation made? Did the investigator make a disclosure of his or her orientation or assumptions?" (p. 99). These judgmental criteria and their subcriteria are intended to evaluate the degree of what is generally called credibility or what is claimed to be truthful.

What makes Stiles' (1999) strategy unique with regard to EQR is "validity criteria" (p. 100), which is mainly concerned with who would have the impact of interpretation and with how the impact of interpretation is utilized and for what purpose. This 3 × 2 grid analysis tool involves three different stakeholders and two different purposes of interpretation. For example, if the purpose of interpretation is to inform the readers of their agreement with regard to what is found in the research, then one major criterion should be *coherence*, which includes follow-up questions such as "Is the interpretation internally consistent? Is it comprehensive? . . . Does it encompass all of the relevant elements and the relations between elements?" (p. 100). If the purpose of interpretation is to make the readers rethink their existing belief system, then the readers should be given *revealing* or *self-evident* learning experiences as they read a text. Subquestions related to this level of evaluation include "Is the interpretation a solution to the concern that motivated the reader's interest? . . . Did it produce change or growth in the reader's perspective? Did it lead to action?" (p. 100).

Regarding the level of evaluation criteria to be applied to the participants, the major criterion is *testimony*, which allows the participants to express their voices from their own perspectives. Follow-up questions are "Did participants indicate that the interpretation accurately described their experience? . . . Were their reactions to hearing the interpretation consistent with the interpretation's motifs? Did they reveal fresh and deeper material?" (Stiles, 1999, p. 100). Catalytic validity, one of Guba and Lincoln's (1989) five authenticity criteria, is used if the purpose of interpretation is to empower the participants' life worlds and to have them "take more control of their lives" (Stiles, 1999, p. 100). This catalytic validity is also more purposefully and critically used in emancipatory social science research—for example, feminist research, neo-Marxist critical ethnography, and Freirian research (Lather, 1993). In effect, Lather (1986) radically redefines catalytic validity as indicating "not only on a recognition of the reality-altering impact of the research process itself, but also on the need to consciously channel this impact so that respondents gain self-understanding and, ideally, self-determination through research participation" (p. 67).

An Art-Based Research Category

Barone and Eisner (2012) note with some critical comment on existing inquiry into EQR that "employing a quantitative metric enables one to enumerate or to summarize quantity. . . . Criteria [for art-based qualitative work] are much more slippery" (p. 147). With specific art-based evaluative criteria in mind, they propose the following set of criteria:

- *Incisiveness*: Getting to the heart of a social issue; "permeates the script and production does indeed offer the potential for waking the reader up to a strange world that appears new and yet always existed in the shadowy corners of the city that they had never explored on their own" (p. 149)
- *Concision*: The degree to which research occupies the minimal amount of space; "any additional material simply diminishes the capacity of the piece to achieve that purpose, waters down the power of the work, and hence its effectiveness" (pp. 149–150)
- *Coherence*: The creation of a work of art-based research whose features hang together as a strong form (pp. 150–151)
- *Generativity*: The ways in which the work enables one to see or act upon phenomena, even though it represents a kind of case study with an *n* of only 1 (pp. 151–152)
- *Social significance*: Something that matters, ideas that count, and important questions to be raised (p. 153)
- *Evocation and illumination*: Feeling or defamiliarizing an object so that it can be seen in a way that is entirely different than the ways in which customary modes of perception operate (p. 154)

Barone and Eisner (2012) add that these six criteria should be seen as "a cue for perception" (p. 154) that assists observers or audiences in making a better evaluation of an art product. Therefore, they offer these criteria merely as a starting point for thinking about the appraisal of works of art-based research. Getting locked into criteria that constrain innovation and that dampen imagination is undesirable. Barone and Eisner take a deliberative, balanced perspective on EQR:

We do not believe that we can have an effective arts based research program without some degree of common reflection over what might be attended to in looking at such work. Thus, in a certain sense, we compromise between, on the one hand, common criteria and, on the other, criteria that are idiosyncratic to the work itself. This may appear a dilemma, but it is a reality. (p. 155)

The compromise alluded to previously is indeed a reality that those involved in qualitative research deal with. Viewing qualitative research as art is not new. Following a recipe book involves the means and the sequence needed to produce a chocolate cake to a particular standard. The problem is, "the more detailed and prescriptive the recipe, the more likely that the cakes made from that recipe will be indistinguishable from one another" (Barone & Eisner, 2012, p. 155). Barone and Eisner "invite you, the readers, to use your own judgment in applying these criteria to the examples of the works of arts based research" (p. 155).

Cho and Trent (2009) suggest validity criteria for assessing performance-related studies (Table 2.2). Performance is often viewed as an "object" or the presentation of the results of analysis (Hamera & Conquergood, 2006, p. 420). In this view, qualitative researchers think, plan, select, and show through performance their inquiry findings as the last phase of assignment/research project completion. Although Cho and Trent support this traditional role for performance in qualitative research, they claim that their conceptualization is broader and incorporates performance aspects at all stages of the inquiry process. They acknowledge the meaning of performance both *in* and *as* qualitative research because the boundary between performance and qualitative research blurs as researchers/teachers and students/audience or researchers and reviewers come to see *conducting qualitative research* as an inevitably personal, social, and political performative process. They advocate for in-depth dialogues and scaffolding to support audiences' and other researchers' introduction to the possibility of constructing and utilizing performance in/as qualitative inquiry (Hamera, 2006; Stucky & Wimmer, 2002).

Pre-performance as imaginative is an ongoing textual rehearsal process as the researcher finalizes the analysis and interpretation

Table 2.2

Validity Criteria Designed to Guide the Development, Enactment, and Assessment of Dialogical Performance of Possibilities

	Pre-Performance	During Performance	Post-Performance
Process	Imaginative Textual rehearsal	Artistic representation Situated engagement	Co-reflexive member checking Caring/ empowered/ nonviolent

Major criteria	Data sufficiency
	Critical interpretation
	Script craftsmanship
	  Multiple voices
	  Persuasive
	  Advocacy
		Aesthetic
		Dialogical engagement
		Understandability
		  Improvisational
		  Empathetic/ authentic
			Divergent reactions
			Focus on major concrete issues
			Generation of possible solutions
			Co-construction of further questions
			Un/learning about social justice
			Promotion of continued conversation and action

Source: Cho, J., & Trent, A. (2009). Validity criteria for performance-related qualitative work: Toward a reflexive, evaluative, and co-constructive framework for performance in/as qualitative inquiry. *Qualitative Inquiry*, *15*(6), 1013–1041.

of the data collected. The focus of imaginative rehearsal is on making the voices of subjects relational and evocative as the researcher constructs texts as scripts. Criteria needed to evaluate this imaginative textual practice involve data sufficiency, level of critical interpretation, and degree of script craftsmanship. The stage of performance-in-use, associated with artistic re/presentation, involves transacting the lived experiences of others to audiences by means of voices and bodies of the performers. One of the main criteria is the degree of understandability of the performance being re/presented. With clear delivery in mind, this criterion is one that cautions that some performance is too complex to understand. Also, the post-performance stage is nurtured by a co-reflexive member-checking process among subjects, performers, and audiences. It is important to link artistic re/presentation with degrees of intensive experience and closeness between the performer and the audience. Post-performance is seen as a beginning, not an ending, because the effect of a performance on the performer and the audience may be rearranged as both parties share their understandings with one another. The performer should be very clear about his or her rationale for checking validity: Whose authority? Whose artistic achievements? Whose evaluative validity is of most importance at this time in this place? Which choices promote the primary aim of attaining a deeper, empathic understanding across participants (both performers and audience members)? These co-constructive validity-seeking questions may help the audiences reflect critically not so much on aesthetics at the surface level as on hidden messages underpinning the performance.

A Post-Validity Category

Before explaining this last category, clarifying the difference between a general sense of credibility used in qualitative research and a theoretical sense of validity classified in this section is needed. The aforementioned four categories of EQR are more or less direct, straightforward, or less abstract in suggesting ways of judging quality or goodness criteria on qualitative research. This post-validity category has its roots in Patti Lather's (1986) seminal article, "Issues of Validity in Openly Ideological Research: Between a Rock and a Soft Place," in which she redefines goodness criteria in ways that make evaluation meaningful for value-based research programs such as feminist research, neo-Marxist ethnography, and Freirian empowering research. She argues that for these research programs to be properly assessed, goodness criteria such as triangulation, construct validity, face validity, and catalytic validity must be built into research designs. That is, critical research programs need accurate data credibility, a researcher's systematized reflexivity, respect for participants' interpretation of data called member-checking, and evidence of participants' change of consciousness.

Scheurich's (1996) article, "The Mask of Validity: A Deconstructive Investigation," takes Lather's critical or value-based research programs a step further to a point where he argues that the conventional approach and Lincoln and Guba's (1985) naturalistic approach are fundamentally similar. That is, general techniques that Lincoln and Guba invented have the same orthodox voices that originated from the positivist paradigm. Social transformational research is validated in ways that require a celebration of the play of multiplicity and difference in data collection, analysis, and interpretation. All in all, EQR in this regard is subject to locality or contextuality in which meaning is de/reconstructed toward social justice.

Here, I discuss an example of this post-validity category. Table 2.3 presents a review form for the journal *Multicultural Perspectives*. This journal accepts both quantitative and qualitative work, but it mostly includes qualitative research articles.

This evaluation rubric to review journal articles in the context of multiculturalism (race, gender, ethnicity, etc.) and multicultural education includes multidimensions that deal with *general thematic criteria*, which are different from generally encountered criteria such as questions, purposes, literature, analysis, and conclusion. Given a number of different notions of multiculturalism and multicultural education, this journal's evaluation rubric adopts such general thematic criteria as provocative content (new and thought-provoking), organized/focused, clear/comprehensive, or interesting reading, along with commonly addressed criteria such as significant topic, clear purpose/scope, methods, and appropriateness to the journal. This review rubric, or general thematic rubric, with nine dimensions/criteria, not only assists reviewers in evaluating broad ranges of research articles submitted to this interdisciplinary journal but also seeks high-quality journal articles by emphasizing strong qualitative evaluation criteria that is "new and thought-provoking."

A Holistic View of EQR

I am aware of the fact that being holistic may mean different things to different people. From a deconstructive perspective (Scheurich, 1996), an endless search for multiple meanings is desirable. I try to make a simple point that being holistic in searching for EQR is just another "new" beginning, not an ending. During the past

Table 2.3
Multicultural Perspectives' Review Guide

Rating Dimension	Ex	G	M	W	Comments
Significant Topic					
Clear Purpose and Scope					
Provocative Content (new and thought-provoking)					
Analytical (theoretical, empirical, conceptual, philosophical)					
Organized and Focused					
Clear and Comprehensive					
Conclusions Valid					
Interesting Reading					
Appropriate for *Multicultural Perspectives*					
Written Comments:					

Directions: Place an "X" for each dimension: **Ex** = Excellent; **G** = Good; **M** = Marginal; **W** = Weak. Jot notes in the "comments" section and incorporate these into the narrative.

several decades, many scholars—such as Joe Maxwell, Patti Lather, Clive Seale, and Martyn Hammersley—have attempted to explore newer senses of validity. As with this line of scholarship, I find myself always amazed at how creative it is for these scholars to come up with meanings, ideas, platforms, or metaphors. In searching for a legitimacy between text and visual images in seeking validity in her autoethnography, Watson (2009) makes the following remark: Many validity theories themselves are "a line of flight, an invitation to further thought rather than an instrument per se" (p. 528). Every EQR theory, just like any other theory, is double-edged, with positive and negative sides. Perhaps, my EQR theorizing effort is likely to continue to evolve in divergent ways as qualitative inquiry gets richer in nature and expands in scope.

Here, I share a story. Six doctoral students in my Advanced Qualitative Research Methods class conducted a small class project in which they explored a current development of EQR in their own fields of study, such as Adult Learning and Technology, Curriculum and Instruction, and Counselor Education. Each identified 2 or 3 current dissertations and research articles related to their interests. Articles for review must have been published in top-tier journals. As such, they identified 11 dissertations from 2001 to 2009. Ten articles selected were published during the period from 2003 to 2009. Their readings were focused on assessing methodology chapters to develop a way to make an overall quality judgment of dissertations and articles.

The following line of reflection on EQR by one of the students is worth mentioning. She reviewed Maxwell's (1992) evaluative validity typology:

> I think that Maxwell presents a great idea in the sense that all researchers should have a process of evaluative validity. However, it should be a more constant evaluation throughout the entire process of the study. It should not just be done at the end. I think of this idea similar to the process of data collection and analysis. Data collection and analysis takes place simultaneously. . . . They should be happening together. I think that member checking is a process that should be evaluated also. . . . Depending on the study, member checking may or may not increase validity. . . . When participants may be shed in a negative light, member checking may not be a way to increase the validity of the study. Researchers should be aware of the tools they use to promote validity within their studies and a good way to do this is to evaluate research processes throughout the entire study.

This reflective comment addresses a necessity for a holistic approach to EQR in terms of a continuing, ongoing, recursive process of data collection, analysis, interpretation, and member checking. This is the practice that we, qualitative researchers, are supposed to do, yet the question is, How seriously and critically do we implement these processes? Furthermore, how seriously and critically do we expect our participants to engage in member checking? Questions, curiosity, and even fear are creeping into our heads. This is just because I believe what Lather (1993) argues about validity as an ideological EQR: "Validity is one that can neither be avoided nor resolved" (p. 674) in qualitative research. Those who are in the camp of positivist or post-positivist EQR believe that they are able to make a quality judgment in a straightforward way. In contrast, those who are in the camp of critical or post-validity EQR may believe that a predetermined set of evaluative criteria would not work to make a quality judgment of a research product. Following Lather's point of view, I argue that EQR can neither be predetermined in theory nor endless in practice. Just as believing a single "Truth" wholeheartedly is dangerous, so is taking politics into account too heavily. A holistic view of EQR is located somewhere between these extreme stances.

Here, I share a sense of holistic EQR I derived from a total of 21 dissertations and empirical research articles. Although the number of sources is small, I believe it is still worth investigating to obtain some insight into the ways in which EQR can be theorized holistically. I made the following eight overarching observations:

1. The selection of 21 studies demonstrated a variety of validity checking methods—for example, member checking, triangulation, transparency, researcher journal, auditing, and collaboration.
2. These methods differed drastically among studies.
3. Relatively speaking, dissertation studies were more concerned with validity compared to journal articles.
4. Not all studies adopted member checking.
5. Almost all studies mentioned triangulation.
6. Use of self-reflexivity and keeping researcher journals appeared to be less utilized.
7. Some studies placed great emphasis on auditing or peer debriefing.
8. Validity in mixed methods is not so much established in practice as it is in developmental stages.

Based on the previous list, the following observations surprised me:

1. I was *most* surprised that two particular articles did not even mention any of the crucial validity methods other than providing some detailed descriptions of the context and participants. In relation to this, many studies considered member checking an option.
2. I was *just* surprised that, with some exceptions, many seemed to consider triangulation as a checklist. This

reminds me of Hammersley's (2008) chapter, "Troubles with Triangulation," in which he examines four kinds of accuracy-driven and multiplicity-based approaches to triangulation.

3. I was *least* surprised that there was little evidence on adopting what one knows about EQR in mixed methods research. This reminds me of Tashakkori and Teddlie's (2008) effort on conceptualizing a mixed methods version of validity. However, I am unable to endorse their integrative framework because it is nothing but a neopositivist (or hybrid post-positivist) framework in favor of logics, inference, and techniques, which derive directly from both conventional validity criteria and basic techniques formulated by Lincoln and Guba in 1985.

What do all these observations mean to me? Not surprisingly, great emphasis is placed on transactional approaches to EQR (techniques are overemphasized), and transformational approaches to EQR are scant (role of reflexivity is undermined). To me, it seems like there is a menu from which to choose. In it, some are required and others elective. A researcher considers some techniques from a list of required and elective ones. Unfortunately, what is most popular is not necessarily what is right. EQR is likely to be idiosyncratic. This is why a holistic approach to evaluative validity is needed. EQR-in-practice should be seen as neither a checklist nor a menu. It should be holistic in nature. My holistic approach to EQR does not seek a complete sense of convergence. It leaves some room as unknown territory that appears never to be reached by the researcher.

Before sharing the beehive metaphor, I review a recent development in how to assess qualitative research in a comprehensive and holistic way. Scholars continue the conversation about evaluating research. Tracy (2010) presents a proposal for a model to ensure *excellent qualitative research*. Tracy's model is a solid synthesis of what has been researched and theorized about in recent history. Alternatively, Lichtman's (2006, 2014) review of EQR includes *personal criteria*, which are based on her philosophy and assumptions regarding a good piece of qualitative research. That is, Lichtman (2006) attempts to make her personal philosophy explicit by reflecting on the self, the other, and the interaction of the self/other. Lichtman (2006) argues that "an understanding of the other does not come about without an understanding of the self and how the self and other connect" (p. 192). She goes on to state, "I believe each is transformed through this research process" (p. 192). In contrast, Tracy (2010) takes an objective stance in establishing her model's rationale for education establishment *power holders*:

> In addition to providing a parsimonious pedagogical tool, I hope my conceptualization may aid in garnering respect for qualitative methods from power holders who know little about our work. Despite the gains of qualitative research in the late 20th century, a methodological conservatism has crept upon social science over the last 10 years . . . evidenced in governmental and funding agencies' preference for research that is quantitative, experimental, and statistically generalizable. . . . High ranking decision makers—in powerful governmental, funding, and institutional review board positions—are *often unprepared and unable to appropriately evaluate qualitative analyses that feature ethnography, case study, and naturalistic data.* (pp. 837–838, emphasis added)

With these pedagogical and political purposes in mind, Tracy (2010) provides eight *universal* hallmarks for high-quality qualitative methods across paradigms, suggesting that each criterion of quality can be approached via a variety of paths and crafts, the combination of which depends on the specific researcher, context, theoretical affiliation, and project. Her eight "big-tent" criteria for excellent qualitative research are provided in Table 2.4.

I examine two of these criteria, "rich rigor" and "meaningful coherence," for clarification. The tricky nature of rigor is a case that may show a complex set of meanings to the evaluators. Rigor in qualitative research is different than in quantitative research. It literally means stiffness, from the Latin word *rigere* (to be stiff), and implies rigidity, harshness, strict precision, unyielding, or inflexibility. The term *qualitative rigor* itself then is an oxymoron, considering that qualitative research is "a journey of explanation and discovery that does not lead to stiff boundaries" (Thomas & Magilvy, 2011, p. 151). To be certain, the word *rigor* involves many dimensions to be considered. In qualitative research, rigor often refers to the thorough ethical conduct of a study of a social phenomenon. I argue that all criteria, rigor and the numerous others, used (or considered) in evaluating qualitative research are

Table 2.4

Eight "Big-Tent" Criteria for Excellent Qualitative Research

Criteria for Quality	Various Means, Practices, and Methods Through Which to Achieve (End Goal)
Worthy topic	The topic of the research • Relevant • Timely • Significant • Interesting
Rich rigor	The study uses sufficient, abundant, appropriate, and complex • Theoretical constructs • Data and time in the field • Sample(s) • Context(s) • Data collection and analysis processes
Sincerity	The study is characterized by • Self-reflexivity about subjective values, biases, and inclinations of the researcher(s) • Transparency about the methods and challenges
Credibility	The research is marked by • Thick description, concrete detail, explication of tacit (nontextual) knowledge, and showing rather than telling • Triangulation or crystallization • Multivocality • Member reflections
Resonance	The research influences, affects, or moves particular readers or a variety of audiences through • Aesthetic, evocative representation • Naturalistic generalizations • Transferable findings

Table 2.4
Continued

Criteria for Quality	Various Means, Practices, and Methods Through Which to Achieve (End Goal)
Significant contribution	The research provides a significant contribution • Conceptually/theoretically • Practically • Morally • Methodologically • Heuristically
Ethical	The research considers • Procedural ethics (such as human subjects) • Situational and culturally specific ethics • Relational ethics • Exiting ethics (leaving the scene and sharing the research)
Meaningful coherence	The study • Achieves what it purports to be about • Uses methods and procedures that fit its stated goals • Meaningfully interconnects literature, research questions/foci, findings, and interpretations with each

Source: Tracy, S. (2010). Qualitative quality: Eight "big- tent" criteria for excellent qualitative research. *Qualitative Inquiry, 16*(10), 837–851.

necessary but may not be sufficient. Tracy's (2010) thesis, therefore, is in line with the tricky nature of rigor, which also reflects what Richardson (2000) mentioned—a wish to have a social science art form of EQR. Tracy continues:

Like all components in this conceptualization—rich rigor is a *necessary but not sufficient* marker of qualitative quality. For qualitative research to be of high quality, it *must* be rigorous. However, a head full of theories and a case full of data does not automatically result in high quality work. Qualitative methodology is as much art as it is effort, piles of data, and time in the field. And just like following a recipe does not guarantee perfect presentation, or completing a vigorous training plan does not guarantee race-day success, rigor does not guarantee a brilliant final product. That being said, rigor does increase the odds for high quality, and the methodological craft skills developed through rigorous practice transcend any single research project, providing a base of qualitative fitness that may enrich future projects. (p. 841, emphasis in original)

Tracy (2010) uses a metaphor of art and recipe to note the fact that a claim for being rigorous involves *a closer investigation*. Its promise and limitation coexist. Importantly, I identify the politics of being rigorous in research at large. The politics of being rigorous is clearly evident in many types of qualitative research. Likewise, techniques to ensure "rigor," such as advanced statistical analyses, do not guarantee a brilliant quantitative research, either. It is all about the perception of reviewers or assessors as to what makes research "good research." All judgment calls involve complex relative, contextual, political, and/or ethical criteria. In this regard, "tools, frameworks, and criteria are not value free" (p. 838).

Meaningful coherence, Tracy's (2010) final criterion, is accomplished when "the study achieves what it purports to be about, uses methods and procedures that fit its stated goals, and meaningfully interconnects literature, research questions/foci, findings, and interpretations with each" (p. 839). This criterion is likely to be seen as a summary of overall judgment in a typical evaluation tool.

Tracy's (2010) "big-tent" set of criteria is a synthesis of other scholars' constructions of existing goodness criteria. These criteria may usefully remind reviewers about a variety of judgmental aspects in their attempts to determine "How good is good enough?" However, it is also important to think about the fact that they "should not be mechanically scored and summed insofar as some issues may be far more important than others in particular studies" (Stiles, 1999, p. 100). In the end, there is a necessity to develop this kind of standardized form of evaluative criteria to be used in qualitative research. Such constructions provide us with meaningful evaluation tools or guidelines, aligned with key criteria, by which to determine degrees of credibility of qualitative research. However, is it really possible to develop standardized forms of evaluation applicable to any type of qualitative research? Tracy thinks it is possible:

Perhaps the most controversial part of this conceptualization is the notion of universal criteria for qualitative quality. However, I believe that we need not be so tied to epistemology or ontology (or the philosophy of the world) that we cannot agree on several common end goals of good qualitative research. Qualitative methodologists range across postpositivist, critical, interpretive, and poststructural communities. In contrast, . . . researcher reflexivity is a validity procedure clearly positioned within the critical paradigm where individuals reflect on the social, cultural, and historical forces that shape their interpretation. . . . I would argue instead that researcher reflexivity—like many other practices for goodness—serves as an important means toward sincerity for research in a number of paradigms. Its utility need not be bound only to critical research. (p. 849)

Re/thinking about the evaluation of qualitative research is an exciting journey full of new ideas, challenges, power, politics, and creativity. As more examples and practices of EQR in many different fields of study are explored in the following chapters, I hope that the reader will have the same feeling about EQR as I do now. Evaluation is an act that involves value or quality judgment that is inseparable from humans. Qualitative research employs the researcher as a key instrument in collecting, analyzing, and interpreting data. EQR is multidimensional. In many cases, research participants are asked to make judgments on not only what they said and showed but also the overall quality of the research. At this time, it is the researcher who faces ethics in terms of the extent to which to address participants' assessment of the process and product of his or her research. Literally, one should ask oneself, "Who owns this research?"

Then, the evaluators—such as master's or dissertation committee members, journal reviewers, or funding agents—play a whole different ball game by not only using given assessment guidelines but also utilizing their own personal, professional knowledge. EQR is a process of constant presentations and representations that tighten goals, processes, outcomes, and impact together toward a better understanding of social worlds. At last, multicultural readers are faced with another level of EQR. Taken together, different paradigmatic stances require different degrees and levels of evaluation elements and processes. I make sense of EQR, namely *hexagonal EQR*, through a beehive metaphor (Figure 2.1).

The shape of a hexagon is naturalistic. Beehives, snowflakes, and molecules are examples that can be found in nature. I like the hexagonal shape because it seems to represent balance. A triangle implies a sense of absolute stability or a function of geometric equilibrium. A hexagon shows a sense of balance or harmony, particularly when it is connected with others. It looks complicated and messy at a distance but patterned and organized when closely seen. Imagine bees constantly moving around the surface of beehives. A beehive is constructed in compactly connected hexagons as bees diligently work with beeswax using their bodies. This analogy can lead qualitative researchers to be more creative in their practical engagement with validity. The shape of a hexagon is unique in that it leads to harmony and balance as it is tightened from and connected to other hexagons.

Cho and Trent's (2006) holistic approach to EQR is characterized by a sense of the hexagon that cuts across all existing "do or don't techniques" (transactional) and "reflexivity-based, collaborative dialogue" (transformational) toward a harmonized, balanced integrative approach to validity. For example, the meaning attached to a beehive involves an interconnection between form and content or between procedures and "ethics in practice" (Guillemin & Gillam, 2004, p. 261). Lather (2007) states that

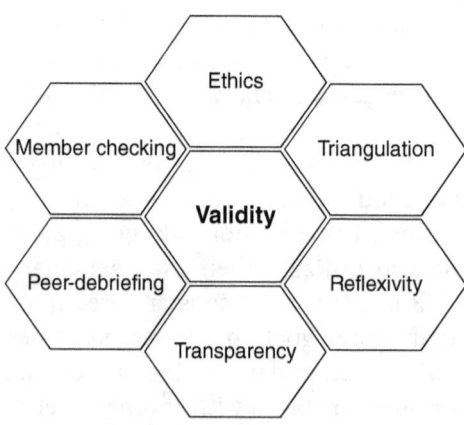

Figure 2.1 Hexagonal EQR.

in order to be intelligible, we need to repeat the familiar and normalized. That task is not whether to repeat but how to repeat it in such a way that repetition displaces that which enables it. (p. 39)

To be more intelligent, I believe I have to constantly be adaptive to a newer line of thought, philosophically and practically. Watson's (2009) picturing validity is a case in which the author, drawing on postmodern realism, creates a newer relational understanding between text and image. Madrid's (2007) attempt to explore "video revisiting" with preschoolers is another case in which the author creates a member-checking procedure appropriate for the specific participants. Double-edged problems of validity fall on the continuum between a *thin* descriptive study on one end and a *thick* descriptive study on the other end. The amount of time and the number of interviews cannot be absolute, determinate validity criteria. Nor can rules-seeking analytical techniques. And a postmodern tale itself cannot be justified as is.

EQR is neither unitary nor paradigm-idiosyncratic. A crucial key criterion is what Geertz (1998) mentions as *deeply hanging out*. Like a bee that intuitively and holistically dances around and filters pollen into beeswax to construct a hive, a qualitative researcher deeply embraces both data and ethics to clearly ensure rigor/intimacy as he or she filters and constructs a balanced story for individual/social justice at varying levels.

Riessman's (2008) reflection on truths and cautions is meaningful in putting the puzzle pieces together:

I prefer not to think in terms of standards or criteria, and warn students away from the "paradigm warfare" that exists out there in the literature. It can paralyze and . . . simplify what are complex validation and ethical issues all investigators face. . . . Narrative truths are always partial—committed and incomplete. (pp. 185–186)

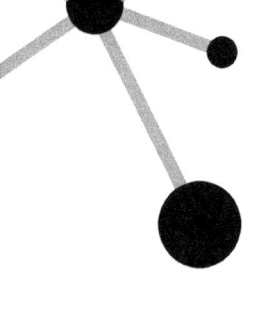

3

PRACTICAL EVALUATION TOOLS AND USES

Introduction

This chapter introduces a number of practical evaluation tools for judging the quality of qualitative research. As noted previously, the field of qualitative research has many different intellectual traditions and disciplinary areas. Thus, it is interdisciplinary and multidisciplinary in nature. Given the belief that an ideal paradigm or model exists out there, I conducted some inquiry into research journals by asking editors to share their assessment tools or guidelines. Almost all editors graciously shared them or provided sound rationales for not having them in place. I believe all of these evaluation tools used in research journals are socially constructed outcomes, which may continue to evolve in the near future. In this chapter, I first briefly discuss research standards of the American Educational Research Association (AERA). AERA is the world's largest educational research association, and it has many research paradigms. By examining its research standards and proposal assessment tools, I uncover the contemporary nature of what makes research good research. Next, I discuss *qualitative touchstones*, which were used in an edited book titled *Reviewing Qualitative Research* (Trainor & Graue, 2013). Qualitative touchstones serve as guiding questions in the context of hypothetically examining the quality of qualitative research. I then specifically examine actual evaluation tools or review guides, from more than 20 contemporary qualitative research journals, for reviewers. Finally, I analyze all these theoretical and practical approaches by comparing and contrasting their essential ideas. Consequently, a holistic analysis table is constructed as I take all evaluative criteria into account. I conclude the chapter with a discussion of a relatively recent assessment model (Gómez, 2009) in which three concrete assessment factors—criteria, process, and writing—are illustrated in an interactive manner.

American Educational Research Association: Research Standards and Descriptive/Prescriptive Rating Scales

A rigorous attempt to identify a set of general checklist criteria embedded in a linear sense of logic, specificity, and thoroughness is clearly evident in the publication of AERA's (2006) "Standards for Reporting on Empirical Social Science Research." AERA uses the word "Standards" and organizes two overarching themes, *warrantability* and *transparency*. Table 3.1 provides an excerpt of the AERA research standards, with a great emphasis on analysis and interpretation.

The general research standards on the left column in Table 3.1 deal with reliability, analysis methods, inference, and conclusions. In the right column for qualitative research, the specific standards focus largely on analysis and interpretation and are strongly geared toward the evidence that serves as a warrant for each claim; practices used to develop and enhance the warrant for the claims; interpretive commentary; and "being transparent" in the process of developing the descriptions, claims, and interpretations. Presumably, these two core themes—warrantability and transparency—which have been proclaimed by the world's largest educational research association, have significantly impacted the qualitative research community in many ways. Warranted claims and transparent procedures could be construed as political in nature and have been used in recent years in the name of scientific, evidence-based research by political conservatives typically thought to oppose the use and funding of qualitative research (Denzin, 2012). On the other hand, many qualitative researchers appear to endorse

Table 3.1

AERA's Standards for Reporting on Empirical Social Science Research

General Research Standards	Qualitative Standards Intended to Make the Process of Analysis Transparent for Reviewers and Readers
5.1. The *procedures used for analysis* should be precisely and transparently described from the beginning of the study through presentation of the outcomes. Reporting should make clear how the analysis procedures address the research question or problem and lead to the outcomes reported. The relevance of the analysis procedures to the problem formulation should be made clear.	5.11. The *process of developing the descriptions, claims, and interpretations* should be clearly described and illustrated. The description should make it possible to follow the course of decisions about the pattern descriptions, claims, and interpretations from the beginning to the end of the analysis process. Sufficient detail should be included to make the process transparent and engender confidence that the results are warranted.
5.2. *Analytic techniques* should be described in sufficient detail to permit understanding of how the data were analyzed and the processes and assumptions underlying specific techniques (e.g., techniques used to undertake content analysis, discourse or text analysis, deliberation analysis, time use analysis, network analysis, or event history analysis).	5.12. The *evidence that serves as a warrant for each claim* should be presented. The sources of evidence and the strength and variety of evidence supporting each claim should be described. Qualifications and conditions should be specified; significant counter-examples should be reported. Claims should be illustrated with concrete examples (e.g., field note excerpts, interview quotes, or narrative vignettes) and descriptions of the social context in which they occurred should be provided. If a warranted claim entails a generalizing statement (e.g., of typicality), it should be supported with evidence of its relative frequency. Speculations that go beyond the available evidence should be clearly represented as such.

(continued)

Table 3.1
Continued

General Research Standards	Qualitative Standards Intended to Make the Process of Analysis Transparent for Reviewers and Readers
5.3. The analysis and presentation of the outcomes of the analysis should make clear how they *support claims or conclusions* drawn in the research.	5.13. *Practices used to develop and enhance the warrant for the claims* should be described, including the search for disconfirming evidence and alternative interpretations of the same evidence. Significant limitations due, for instance, to insufficient or conflicting evidence, should be described.
5.4. Analysis and interpretation should include information about any *intended or unintended circumstances* that may have significant implications for interpretation of the outcomes, limit their applicability, or compromise their validity. Such circumstances may include, but are not limited to, key actors leaving the site, changes in membership of the group, or withdrawal of access to any part of the study or to people in the study.	5.14. *Interpretive commentary* should provide a deeper understanding of the claims—how and why the patterns described may have occurred; the social, cultural, or historical contexts in which they occurred; how they relate to one another; how they relate to (support or challenge) theory and findings from previous research; and what alternative claims or counter-claims were considered.
5.5. The *presentation of conclusions* should (a) provide a statement of how claims and interpretations address the research problem, question, or issue underlying the research; (b) show how the conclusions connect to support, elaborate, or challenge conclusions in earlier scholarship; and (c) emphasize the theoretical, practical, or methodological implications of the study.	

Source: American Educational Research Association (2006, pp. 37–38).

the word "transparency" as a newly emergent important criterion in conducting and evaluating qualitative research.

Table 3.2 presents a review form for evaluating the annual AERA conference proposals. It addresses the research standards alluded to previously by specifying warrantability and transparency. The evaluation contents or criteria of this review form are aligned with general research procedures, just like those of checklists, but they are much more descriptive and prescriptive. The form describes each research component (e.g., perspectives or theoretical framework) and also prescribes what must be expected by a reviewer (e.g., evidence, substantiation or warrants for arguments, and scientific significance). In addition, it gives a scale of ratings from 1 to 5. It is typical that reviewers are eventually asked to make a decision. To my knowledge, providing written comments is typical, along with a decision that falls within one of four judgmental calls: accepted as is, accepted with minor revision, accepted with major revision, and reject. The AERA proposal review evaluation form has a binary decision rule—accepted or rejected—and includes comments for both writer and Division Chair.

Touchstones for Reviewing Qualitative Research

Trainor and Graue (2013) pay attention to Hancock and Mueller's (2010) *Reviewer's Guide to Quantitative Methods in the Social Sciences*, wonder if reviewers in qualitative research would need such a guideline, and question a necessity for a common set of assumptions or tools for qualitative inquiry. After having live discussions with other qualitative researchers, Trainor and Graue assert that "devoting consistent attention to the foundational aspects of qualitative research would allow the identification of criteria for quality" (p. 4). I am in agreement with their assertion. This is not because I believe one will find a definite set of criteria for *all* but, rather, because I believe such consistent attention itself is necessary to provide for continuous awareness for *all*. For this reason, I endorse Trainor and Graue's reference to *touchstones* as "parameters for criteria estimating, if not evaluating, the quality of qualitative research" (p. 7). I remind the reader of the words in the statement, "estimating, if not evaluating," here. Touchstones are literally referred to as a criterion or standard by which judgment is made, which can be an addition to my array of qualitative

Table 3.2

AERA's Annual Conference Proposal Review Form

Objectives or Purposes	Min (Insignificant) 1 2 3 4	Max (Critically significant) 5
Perspective(s) or theoretical framework	Min (Not well executed) 1 2 3 4	Max (Well executed) 5
Methods, techniques, or modes of inquiry	Min (Not well executed) 1 2 3 4	Max (Well executed) 5
Data sources, evidence, objects, or materials	Min (Inappropriate) 1 2 3 4	Max (Appropriate) 5
Results and/or substantiated conclusions or warrants for arguments/point of view	Min (Ungrounded) 1 2 3 4	Max (Well grounded) 5
Scientific or scholarly significance of the study or work	Min (Routine) 1 2 3 4	Max (Highly original) 5
Comments to the program chair (This field is mandatory; you must comment)		
Comments to the author/submitter (This field is mandatory; you must comment)		
Reviewer recommendation Accept ( ) Reject ( )		

judgmental words discussed in Chapter 1. As all qualitative research community members know, any simplified indicator that leads to absolute claims about quality is simply undesirable. As Trainor and Graue note, the word "touchstone" serves as a space in which other key qualitative words, such as "creativity," "balance," or "flexibility" (p. 8), can be wisely used. After presenting a set of touchstones in different types of qualitative research, I add my comments.

Twelve kinds of qualitative research are introduced in Trainor and Graue's (2013) seminal book:

1. Action research
2. Autoethnography
3. Case studies
4. Critical discourse analysis
5. Ethnography
6. The grounded theory method
7. Interview research
8. Oral history/life history/biography
9. Narrative inquiry
10. Phenomenology
11. Poetics and performance
12. Positional and identity-based theories of research

The reader is encouraged to refer to Trainor and Graue's book to learn more about each set of touchstones in accordance with each kind of qualitative research. In particular, it is worth paying attention to the ways in which the contributors to their book rationalize theoretical underpinnings of the touchstones in their chosen qualitative research.

The following section of this chapter covers most of the 12 types of qualitative research in the context of current methodology journals. The three types of qualitative research in Trainor and Graue's (2013) book that are not covered in the next section are oral history/life history/biography, poetics and performance, and positional and identify-based theories of research. Let me briefly explain some of these unique touchstones here.

First, Janesick (2013) proposes four touchstones in oral history/life history/biography as a whole. *Harmony* is the last touchstone that asks, "Are the conclusions and interpretations based on the data presented for study and is the narrative coherent, nuanced, and layered? Are the voices of marginalized individuals included?" (p. 160). The harmony touchstone indicates an overall quality of work that results in proper data interpretation, representation, and conclusion represented by the voice of the people at margin. Second, Prendergast and Belliveau (2013) suggest four different touchstones, each in poetics and performance. These touchstones are so concise and directive that a reviewer can easily apply them to works done artistically and performatively. Criteria used in the assessment of poetics, such as effective, affective, reflexive, impact, and aesthetic and disciplinary, are seen as concrete indicators that illustrate what matters most in the form and content of a poem. As such, performance-related criteria show a robust anchor of what a performance is and should be. A caveat on the assessment of performance may be an absence of social action or social justice-driven criterion. Third, Dixson and Dodo Seriki (2013) demonstrate six touchstones in the position and identity-based theories of research. The first two touchstones with regard to a *researcher's responsibility* and *advocacy* are highly appropriate.

In closing, all these touchstones throughout Trainor and Graue's (2013) edited book are preferably used to estimate, if not evaluate, qualities of qualitative research from a theoretical perspective, leaving the door open for further practical implications. With this in mind, it will be very meaningful to be familiar with actual review guides used in current qualitative research journals. The next section presents examples of these actual review guides.

Evaluation of Contemporary Qualitative Research Journals With or Without Specific Tools or Review Guides

In this section, I examine real review guidelines, including assessment checklists, a series of questions, sets of criteria, or rubrics of contemporary qualitative research journals. As expected, I find two kinds of manuscript evaluations conducted qualitatively—one with no specific guidelines and the other with specific guidelines. I discuss mixed methods research in Chapter 4. Readers are reminded that both evaluation methods are equally useful and meaningful when considering the nature of qualitative research. Indeed, I am mindful of any standardized or prescriptive assessment form that is expected to be utilized in all qualitative research methodologies. Therefore, not having such specific review guidelines is understandable given the different epistemological and methodological differences. Furthermore, whether or not such specific assessment guidelines are available for certain journals also has to do with a decision made by an editor(s) who has a firm belief that select reviewers still provide necessary and sufficient written comments useful to make a decision. That is, there is a strong sense in the qualitative research profession that a great deal of qualitative research journal reviewers still do an excellent job of providing facts and opinions leading to valid decisions to be made by an editor(s), regardless of whether or not they are given guided assessment checklists or rubrics.

Readers should keep in mind that evaluation of qualitative research falls into a plurality of both traditions and practicality. I obtained sources of information on the journals by pulling out almost all the names of qualitative journals (a couple of them accept both quantitative and qualitative research methodologies, along with mixed methods) through *The Qualitative Report*'s website (http://www.nova.edu/ssss/QR) and asking those journal editors if they could share evaluations of qualitative research. Almost all editors graciously and generously replied and provided tools, opinions, and thoughts through e-mails. They are greatly appreciated.

No Specific Tools or Review Guidelines

The following journals, in no particular order, do not use specific assessment tools: *Phenomenology and the Cognitive Sciences, Journal of Phenomenological Psychology, Journal of Qualitative Criminal Justice & Criminology, Journal of Business Anthropology, Narrative Inquiry, Discourse Studies*, and *International Journal of Qualitative Research in Services*. Some correspondences with journal editors are presented next, followed by a summary of the journal editors' statements.

Phenomenology and the Cognitive Sciences

We use an online system for reviewers. There are simply two text boxes—one asking for confidential comments for the editors, and the other asking for comments that we share with authors. No other instructions are given. That is, we don't have a rubric; we depend on quality referees who are experts in their field.

—Shaun Gallagher, PhD (personal
communication, July 14, 2014)

Journal of Phenomenological Psychology

As you may know the *Journal of Phenomenological Psychology* was founded in 1970 and was the first journal in psychology to offer a venue for qualitative research. But the qualitative research we employ is founded upon the phenomenological epistemology granted by continental thought. So while we are clearly identified with the discipline of psychology, we have always maintained a close relationship to primary sources in continental philosophy—specifically Husserl, Heidegger, Sartre and Merleau-Ponty. The Journal (JPP) generally categorizes submissions in 3 categories: theoretical, clinical and empirical. For all categories we employ a double-blind peer review process. For empirical (qualitative) submissions we do ask that the methodology be within the phenomenological scope of our journal. With the rise of so many new qualitative methods we have had to become more selective as most new qualitative methods are primarily "interpretive" and founded on postmodern or constructivist approaches—which do not employ a phenomenological philosophical approach or methodology. Unlike constructivism, phenomenology endorses a positive nomothetic approach to knowledge. Phenomenology is not just ideographic. Also, most of the secondary qualitative textbook literature unfortunately misrepresents phenomenology. So ironically, while we welcomed the rise of new qualitative methods, we also had to learn to screen out qualitative methods that had little or no relation to the scientific project of phenomenological psychology. Compared to most qualitative methodologies, ours could be understood as primarily descriptive. The rigorous line-by-line "meaning unit" data analysis that pays close attention to linguistic detail in descriptive phenomenological research is outlined in Giorgi 1969, 2009, & Wertz, 2011 and others. Space does not permit me to go into detail about the entire data analysis process in the phenomenological method and approach. But the meaning unit method itself makes transparent to the external "expert-other" reader exactly "how and where" the researcher transformed the meanings of the research participant. The descriptive phenomenological method makes the data analysis maximally transparent for critique by others.

So we like to think that "quality control" is built into the method itself. But my general answer to your question is that assessment is performed through our peer review process. Reviewers are selected by the editor for their particular expertise in phenomenological methodology. Sometimes requests are made for raw data, but usually submissions contain enough material to permit the reviewers to discern the quality of the data analysis. As phenomenology is neither inductive nor deductive, but based on the intuitive analysis of essential structures, much of the review process is focused on this latter "essential structure" phase of the research process.

So the direct answer to your question about rubrics is: NO, we do not employ rubrics. Our standards for rigor and quality control are based on the quality and the training of our reviewers.

However, as I have only just taken over the role of Editor-in-Chief, one of my projects is the development of a research manual that would make the methodology more assessable to the general public who may not have a background in the primary philosophical sources of phenomenological psychology. In this manual our writing team will consider the possible use of rubrics for empirical phenomenological research. So your questions are timely to our concerns. Rubrics may be helpful, but they could also be antithetical to phenomenological epistemology. It would depend on the stage of research in which they were applied. It is a question I anticipate raising with my team.

—James Morley, PhD, Editor-in-Chief (personal communication, July 11, 2014)

Journal of Qualitative Criminal Justice & Criminology

Unfortunately, there is nothing I can send you regarding assessment tools or rubrics. The reason is this: I have none. And the reason I have none is because it has been my experience that I get better reviews without them. Qualitative types already approach things differently, so having a bunch of forms or various requirements, I believe, hampers them. I tell my reviewers that they may review however they are most comfortable. Some like to send me an e-mail, some type their responses up, some use bullets, others use track changes, etc. By allowing them the freedom to review how they are most comfortable, I believe I get better reviews. The only other thing I ask is for an editorial recommendation. Here again, rather than forcing them into categories such as revise and resubmit or reject, sometimes I will get responses such as, "This paper gets a very strong revise and resubmit, and there is a good possibility the author(s) may not be able to make all of the necessary revisions, but without all of them, the paper should be rejected." Responses like that are very telling, but you can't get that with pigeon-holed categories. So, my philosophy is that qualitative people are most comfortable with words, let them use words, not quantifiable categories.

—Willard Oliver, PhD (personal
communication, July 11, 2014)

Journal of Business Anthropology

We do not have any format for reviewers to use to evaluate manuscripts—mainly because I do not believe in such tools! Instead, they are asked to write free evaluations, which give an overview of the topic of the paper reviewed, suggest ways to improve the discussion/argument, and make a recommendation (fail, revise and resubmit, etc.). As Editors we consider both reviews and make a judgment on the basis of what they say.

—Brian Moeran (personal communication, July 11, 2014)

Narrative Inquiry

Although I am teaching a course entitled "Qualitative Inquiry," and occasionally also a course entitled "Narrative Inquiry," I really can't give you any firm guidelines the way you may desire. However, in a recent FORUM piece that I put into our journal, I have kind of outlined the criteria for qualitative, narrative analysis—it is called "Why Narrative?" and I've put it on my website.

—Michael Bamberg, PhD (personal
communication, July 11, 2014)

Discourse Studies

I am afraid we have none. All reviewers have their own way of evaluating papers. I am afraid it is not a science. And it depends on the topic, the kind of direction of discourse studies (some very formal and precise others much less so), the country, the data and so on. I do have a mechanism of self-selection ("pre-review") which gives some hints, especially the instruction "What Is Discourse Analysis."

—Teun A. van Dijk, PhD (personal
communication, July, 11, 2014)

International Journal of Qualitative Research in Services

(Unfortunately?) we do not have a standard instrument/rubric to rate journals. I guess that makes sense, given the way we define qualitative research. Yes, Inderscience manuscript submission system has certain standard questions that reviewers should answer (like whether the article contributes to theory, practice, or whether it is relevant for the journal); but, beyond that, we leave it up to the "qualitative judgment" of the reviewers.

—Babu P. George, PhD (personal
communication, July 10, 2014)

Taken together, I created a synthesis of what these journal editors noted (Table 3.3).

As can be seen from Table 3.3, what these seven journal editors expressed in regard to the absence of specific evaluation tools is fundamental in addressing what qualitative research should be. I take all these codes into consideration and derive the following four essential codes:

- Trust
- Freedom
- The nature of qualitative research
- It works

The first aspect has to do with a basic belief system underpinning a sound qualitative research community in which trust must prevail. Given this trusted sense of community, these editors provide

Table 3.3

Journal Editors' Comments on Non-Use of Review Guide

Key Expressions in the Editors' Words	Codes I Develop
"We depend on quality referees who are experts in their field."	1. Credential 2. Trust
"Our standards for rigor and quality control are based on the quality and the training of our reviewers."	3. The quality and the training of our reviewer
"It has been my experience that I get better reviews without them. Qualitative types already approach things differently, so having a bunch of forms or various requirements, I believe, hampers them. By allowing them the freedom to review how they are most comfortable, I believe I get better reviews."	4. Personal/professional experiences 5. Trust 6. Professional conduct 7. No predetermined tool forced 8. Freedom 9. Comfortable to review
"I do not believe in such tools! Instead, they are asked to write free evaluations. All reviewers have their own way of evaluating papers. I am afraid it is not a science. And it depends on the topic."	10. Freedom 11. Their own way 12. Reviewing the quality of qualitative research is not a science 13. Depending on the topic
"We do not have a standard instrument/rubric to rate journals. I guess that makes sense, given the way we define qualitative research."	14. Reviewing the quality of qualitative research is not a science

reviewers with freedom to do their job. The sense of freedom implies implicit responsibility on the shoulders of the reviewers. A detailed written comment is expected for judgment, justification, and decision. The third leads us to make a contrast between science and art. Indeed, qualitative research is art and/or a holistic mix of science and art. Last, these journal editors said that "it has worked"—that is, select reviewers have done their job the way they are expected. If journal editors trust in the credentials and training experiences of the reviewers, provide reviewers with freedom, and remind reviewers of the nature of qualitative research, then they believe they will receive necessary and sufficient reviews that are instrumental for making judgments of manuscripts.

Specific Review Checklist/Rubrics

I have found 11 qualitative journals that use some specific review guidelines such as checklists or rubrics, along with written comments. I add a few journals I know that use some specific review tools. Again, they do not represent all of the qualitative journals available on earth. As noted previously, use of these specific tools does not necessarily mean that reviewers would provide better facts or opinions compared to the non-use of these kinds of tools. Many generous journal editors replied quickly to my request and shared their review tools or guidelines with me. The names of these journals, in no particular order, are as follows: *Action Research Journal, Qualitative Inquiries in Music Therapy: Monograph Series, Narrative Inquiry in Bioethics, SAGE's Reviewer Gateway, International Journal of Qualitative Methods, Cultural Anthropology, Journal of Organizational Ethnography, International Sociology, Equity & Excellence in Education, Journal of Ethnographic and Qualitative Research,* and *Grounded Theory Review: An International Journal.* Here, I make nonjudgmental comments regarding each of these journals and summarize an overall trend of the evaluation of qualitative research in the use of specific tools or review guides.

> *Action Research Journal* (Hilary Bradbury-Huang, PhD, personal communication, July 13, 2014) (Box 3.1)

This review guideline shows what action research is and how it proceeds in a very specific and clear way. A set of seven criteria follows a process that is commonly known in research. In Chapter 2, I examined 10 commonly known research elements and processes: expertise, problem and/or research question, purpose, literature review, context, sample, data collection, data processing and plans for analysis, human subject, and importance to the field. Most criteria are identical. Nonetheless, the advantage of the *Action Research* review guideline is that each criterion has very concise, informative descriptions. Languages used in this guideline are plain and clear, so reviewers can make sense of what exactly they are being asked to do. All these descriptions are greatly relevant to the nature of what action research is generally known as. All in all, with seven concise headings aided by meaningful descriptions, this review guideline provides reviewers with valid and reliable languages, exemplified in the criterion *actionability*, which represents the spirit of action research.

Qualitative Inquiries in Music Therapy: Monograph Series

Our guidelines for authors provide basic criteria for submitting studies for review, and then the editors use the attached review form to determine whether to publish.

—Kenneth E. Bruscia, PhD (personal communication, July 11, 2014) (Box 3.2)

Box 3.1. *Action Research Journal's* Review Guide [Please note that this *Action Research Journal* accepts manuscripts done quantitatively, qualitatively, or mixed-methodically]

....

Quality Criteria for *Action Research Journal*

The following seven criteria are the product of *ARJ* associate editor board members' "collogue" on what constitutes "quality in action research." They represent the criteria upon which there was the highest degree of consensus. Our objective in making these criteria explicit is to be transparent about the qualities that are critical to us as a board of associate editors in evaluating papers. We regard this articulation as a living document that will be reviewed annually. We therefore intend to track the use and usefulness of the criteria for ourselves and our stakeholders. The criteria will replace the set in current use on manuscript central. A much more detailed document about the collogue is available here, along with the *ARJ* submission guidelines, available here.

1. Articulation of objectives

The extent to which the authors explicitly address the objectives they believe relevant to their work and the choices they have made in meeting those.

2. Partnership and participation

The extent to and means by which the paper reflects or enacts participative values and concern for the relational component of research. By the extent of participation we are referring to a continuum from consultation with stakeholders to stakeholders as full co-researchers.

3. Contribution to action research theory/practice

The extent to which the paper builds on (creates explicit links with) or contributes to a wider body of practice knowledge and/or theory, that contributes to the action research literature.

4. Methods and process

The extent to which the action research process and related methods are clearly articulated and illustrated. By illustrated we mean that empirical papers "show" and not just "tell" about process and outcomes by including analysis of data that includes the voices of participants in the research.

5. Actionability

The extent to which the paper provides new ideas that guide action in response to need.

6. Reflexivity

The extent to which self-location as a change agent is acknowledged by the authors. By self-location we mean that authors take a personal, involved, and self-critical stance as reflected in clarity about their role in the action research process, clarity about the context in which the research takes place, and clarity about what led to their involvement in this research.

7. Significance

The extent to which the insights in the manuscript are significant in content and process. By significant we mean having meaning and relevance beyond their immediate context in support of the flourishing of persons, communities, and the wider ecology.

The 10 criteria listed in Box 3.2 address the quality of qualitative monographs in the field of music therapy. I have never encountered an example of music therapy papers and may not be in a position to review this field of study. Nonetheless, here I find a great deal of commonalities with other traditional qualitative research fields: significance, purpose, participant selection, method, ethics, contribution, analysis, write-up, and organization. Three unique aspects of this review guideline are as follows. Initially, the first criterion, "Extent to which study exemplifies qualitative paradigm," gets my attention. It appears that the paradigm discourse in qualitative music therapy

Box 3.2. *Qualitative Inquiries in Music Therapy: Monograph Series*

....

Editorial Review Form

Please address each issue with a brief comment:
- Extent to which study exemplifies qualitative paradigm:
- Significance, relevance, need for study:
- Clarity of focus and purpose:
- Appropriateness of participant selection:
- Appropriateness and responsiveness of method:
- Adherence to ethical guidelines:
- Researcher's awareness of own contributions to findings:
- Relevance of findings to data:
- Clarity of writing:
- Organization of report:

    Other comments:

Suggested Revisions:

Please check one of the following:

____ Definitely publish (minimal revision needed)
____ Publish after revisions have been completed to the satisfaction of Chief Editor.
____ Ask author to revise significant, then re-submit for another review by board.
____ Do not publish.

....

monographs is regarded as highly important. Second, the overall organization and structure of this review guideline is likely to be discipline-specific. Criteria related to methodology are specified in terms of participant selection and methods adopted. Third, ethical consideration is located in the middle of this review guideline, whereas it is typically located at the end of many review guidelines. This implies that qualitative music therapy requires a different way in which ethics is adopted and enforced.

Narrative Inquiry in Bioethics

A relatively new qualitative research journal, *Narrative Inquiry in Bioethics* (*NIB*) provides a forum for exploring current issues in bioethics through personal stories, qualitative and mixed methods research articles, and case studies. *NIB* is dedicated to fostering a deeper understanding of bioethical issues by publishing rich descriptions of complex human experiences written in the words of the person experiencing them (http://www.nibjournal.org/journal). The journal's latest guidelines for authors of qualitative research articles can be accessed at (http://www.nibjournal.org/authors/guidelines.html). This journal encourages those who consider submitting manuscripts to review the COREQ (Consolidated Criteria for Reporting Qualitative Research) guideline (Tong, Sainsbury, & Craig, 2007), which is provided in Table 3.4. It has three larger domains (research team and reflexivity, study design, and analysis and findings) and eight subdomains (personal characteristics, relationship with participants, theoretical framework, participant selection, setting, data collection, data analysis, and reporting) consisting of a 32-item checklist for interview and focus groups. The COREQ health research guideline is designed to explore a number of indicators of excellent qualitative research. In particular, I think that checklists in the sections of data collection, analysis, and reporting provide very concise tips, ideas, and methodical procedures. All necessary and sufficient research endeavors intended to improve the quality of qualitative research are included. One of the editors of this journal asserts that "while the COREQ guidelines focus on what should be reported, they also enable you to consider a wide variety of issues at the front end of a study" (James M. DuBois, PhD, personal communication, July 12, 2014). I found different proposal guidelines for different forms of research presentations and articles on the website, so I present here

Table 3.4

Narrative Inquiry in Bioethics' Review Guide

Domain 1: Research team and reflexivity

Personal characteristics

1	Interviewer/ facilitator	Which author/s conducted the interview or focus group?
2	Credentials	What were the researcher's credentials? E.g. _PhD, MD_
3	Occupation	What was their occupation at the time of the study?
4	Gender	Was the researcher male or female?
5	Experience and training	What experience or training did the researcher have?

Relationship with participants

6	Relationship established	Was a relationship established prior to study commencement?
7	Participant knowledge of the interviewer	What did the participants know about the researcher? E.g. _personal goals, reasons for doing the research_
8	Interviewer characteristics	What characteristics were reported about the interviewer/facilitator? E.g. _bias, assumptions, reasons and interests in the research topic_

Domain 2: Study design

Theoretical framework

9	Methodological orientation and theory	What methodological orientation was stated to underpin the study? E.g. _grounded theory, discourse analysis, ethnography, phenomenology, content analysis_

Table 3.4

Continued

Domain 1: Research team and reflexivity

Participant selection

10	Sampling	How were participants selected? E.g. *purposive, convenience, consecutive, snowball*
11	Method of approach	How were participants approached? E.g. *face-to-face, telephone, mail, e-mail*
12	Sample size	How many participants were in the study?
13	Non-participation	How many people refused to participate or dropped out? Reasons?
Setting		
14	Setting of data collection	Where was the data collected? E.g. *home, clinic, workplace*
15	Presence of non-participants	Was anyone else present besides the participants and researchers?
16	Description of sample	What are the important characteristics of the sample? E.g. *demographic data, date*
Data collection		
17	Interview guide	Were questions, prompts, guides provided by the authors? Was it pilot tested?
18	Repeat interviews	Were repeat interviews carried out? If yes, how many?
19	Audio/visual recording	Did the research use audio or visual recording to collect the data?
20	Field notes	Were field notes made during and/or after the interview or focus group?
21	Duration	What was the duration of the interviews or focus group?

(*continued*)

Table 3.4
Continued

Domain 1: Research team and reflexivity		
22	Data saturation	Was data saturation discussed?
23	Transcripts returned	Were transcripts returned to participants for comment and/or correction?
Domain 3: Analysis and findings		
Data analysis		
24	Number of data coders	How many data coders coded the data?
25	Description of the coding tree	Did authors provide a description of the coding tree?
26	Derivation of themes	Were themes identified in advance or derived from the data?
27	Software	What software, if applicable, was used to manage the data?
28	Participant checking	Did participants provide feedback on the findings?
Reporting		
29	Quotations presented	Were participant quotations presented to illustrate the themes/findings? Was each quotation identified? E.g. *participant number*
30	Data and findings consistent	Was there consistency between the data presented and the findings?
31	Clarity of major themes	Were major themes clearly presented in the findings?
32	Clarity of minor themes	Is there a description of diverse cases or discussion of minor themes?

Source: Tong, A., Sainsbury, P., & Craig, J. (2007). Consolidated Criteria for Reporting Qualitative Research (COREQ): A 32-item checklist for interviews and focus groups. *International Journal of Qualitative Health Care, 19*(6), 349–357.

a few overarching criteria that may interest members of the general qualitative research community:

- What topic do you propose?
- How is it relevant to health care ethics or policy?
- Why is a narrative approach needed?
- What new insights might it provide into the subject matter?
- Describe the kind of person who might write the stories.
- How do you plan to recruit personal stories?
- Do you have personal contacts within the target community?
- Can you access listservs to share a call for stories?
- Will your target group readily have access to e-mail?
- Do you have peers who would assist in recruiting story authors?
- What do you plan to ask authors of personal stories to address and how will you ask them to structure their contributions?

The *NIB* proposal guidelines, assuming that these proposals will be invited for publication consideration later on, pay particular attention to uniqueness, process, and access that indicate the value and validity of human stories that reside in a community. This attention is very legitimate when considering case studies pertaining to a recent issue regarding, for example, living organ donation. Transparency, confidentiality, and community support are key in making narrative inquiry in bioethics successful.

SAGE's Reviewer Gateway

The "Journal Reviewer Gateway" is available on the website of SAGE Publishing Company (http://www.sagepub.com/journal-gateway/reviewerGateway.htm). There are many major qualitative research journals published by SAGE. According to this website, some SAGE journals offer specific review guidelines, whereas others do not. It reads, "If a journal does not offer a structured questionnaire or form for reviewers, it can be useful to think about the following things as you read the paper to help you structure your report." I think this comprehensive reviewer guideline from SAGE is very informative and useful (Box 3.3). Due to space limitations, I highlight a list of keywords or expressions from this lengthy document on the website. The first heading is concerned with an overall quality of the manuscripts in terms of (1) relevancy, (2) significance, (3) originality, (4) methodology, and (5) technical accuracy. The second heading is concerned with the structure and communication of the manuscripts regarding (1) accuracy of references, (2) overall communication and argument, (3) quality of written language, (4) effectiveness of the article abstract and introduction, (5) logical argument and conclusion with supportive evidence, (6) the suitability of the title, (7) the effectiveness of the abstract, (8) the appropriateness of the article type, (9) broad readership, and (10) internal consistency.

The previously mentioned 15 criteria from the first and second headings of SAGE's Reviewer Gateway are convergent with the following key criteria: relevancy, significance, originality, methodology, structure and organization, communication, accuracy, and readership. SAGE's Reviewer Gateway demonstrates two distinct notions of assessing the quality of qualitative research. One is that SAGE's Reviewer Gateway pinpoints specific characteristics of a research article that require external (a title, an abstract, introduction, etc.) and internal (communication, logics, argument, etc.) qualities that are important to be assessed. The other is that the SAGE's Reviewer Gateway explicitly emphasizes the importance of research ethics, particularly in relation to not only research ethics per se but also the review process.

International Journal of Qualitative Methods (Alexander M. Clark, PhD, personal communication, July 11, 2014).

This well-known qualitative research journal provides rich information needed to make the evaluation of qualitative research better understood. The editor of this journal presents two examples. One example is what this journal uses for review (Box 3.4). The other example, developed at the University of Oxford, is a resource that helps reviewers understand the evaluation of qualitative researcher better.

As shown in Box 3.4, the seven criteria deal with a variety of aspects of qualitative research necessary for assessing internal and external qualities. Explanations accompanying these criteria are concise and directive in helping reviewers draw particular attention as effectively as possible. Words such as "overview," "summary," or "comprehensive" are properly used throughout this

Box 3.3. Journal Reviewer Gateway at the website of SAGE Publishing Company

What to look out for and comment on:

- Relevance to the publication
- Significance of the research within the field
- Originality of the work conducted
- The methodology employed during the research
- Technical accuracy

Structure and communication:

- Accuracy of references
- Structure of the paper overall, communication of main points and flow of argument
- Quality of written language and structure of the article
- Effectiveness of the article abstract and introduction
- Whether the argument is clear and logical and the conclusions presented are supported by the results or evidence presented
- Whether the title of the article is suitable or effective
- Whether the abstract is a good summary of the article
- Whether the work meets with the article types accepted by the journal
- The accessibility of the paper to a broad readership
- Whether the paper is internally consistent

Feedback in your reviewer report

Making a decision

Most important—keep all activity, content and comments relating to the paper confidential.

For information on ethics and responsibility and how to act if you suspect that misconduct has taken place, please see the Ethics section of this Gateway and remember to keep your suspicions confidential, between you and the journal editor, at all times.

Box 3.4. *International Journal of Qualitative Methods'*
Review Guide

1. *Background/Study justification/Summary of pilot work:* Give a persuasive overview to justify your study based on past research and theory, followed by details of any pilot work done to date.
2. *Explanation and justification of method:* Give a clear, comprehensive, and detailed overview of which method you used, what you did, and why.
3. *Sampling/Recruitment:* Give a clear, comprehensive, and detailed overview of the people involved in the study, what you did to recruit them, and why.
4. *Data handling/Analysis:* Give a clear, comprehensive, and detailed overview of how you handled and analyzed your data, including how you will handle disagreements and/or team analysis.
5. *Ethics:* Provide a summary of the main ethical issues raised by the study and how these are to be addressed.
6. *Rigour:* Discuss the approach to qualitative rigour to be adopted and the steps to be used to maintain rigour.
7. *Full copies of interview schedules/Focus group schedules/Fieldwork plans:* Include full schedules if possible.

review sheet. In particular, it appears that this review sheet, used at the international level, carefully addresses what the journal looks for, with great emphasis on method or methodology:

- Criterion 1 is for introduction and literature review.
- Criteria 2–5 are for methodology.
- Criterion 6 is for discussion and conclusion.
- Criterion 7 is for supplementary elements related to methods.

It is not surprising that some criteria include a chain of words that cover different elements in a broad division. For example, consider the first criterion, "Background/Study justification/Summary of pilot work." It displays three different sets of words as one criterion. To elaborate, the way this criterion is displayed directly indicates both introduction and literature review prior to methodology in any given research article. The way in which this condensed criterion is adopted to imply two parts of a research journal is unique. Its attached explanation reads, "Give a persuasive overview to justify your study based on past research and theory, followed by details of any pilot work done to date." In a word, this first condensed criterion entails background and literature review. Nonetheless, the next three criteria are devoted to extensively covering methodology from rationale, sampling, data analysis, and ethics. Raising back-to-back "why" questions with regard to rationale and sampling gains my attention. The criterion, Data handling/Analysis, suggests reviewers explore how an author perceives and proceeds in a complex process of data analysis. A notion of ethics is excellent, and I am impressed with the inclusion of the word "rigour" as a distinctive criterion related to interpretation and discussion in this review sheet. Last, asking authors of a qualitative manuscript to attach "Full copies of interview schedules/Focus group schedules/Fieldwork plans" is also a unique and distinctive feature of this international qualitative research journal.

Now, let me briefly discuss CASP (Critical Appraisal Skills Programme), which was developed by the University of Oxford. CASP has 10 questions to help us make sense of qualitative research, which in turn direct the reviewers to be more clear about the evaluation of qualitative research. The following are directions on how to use CASP:

A short version of CASP is presented in Table 3.5.

As noted previously, CASP is a simple two-tiered evaluation tool. The first tier involves two basic questions about research aims and methodology. Assuming that the answer to both questions is "Yes," a reviewer attempts to answer the remaining eight questions, which cover design, recruitment, data collection, power/ rapport, ethics, data analysis, results, and significance. These eight

Three broad issues need to be considered when appraising the report of a qualitative research:

- Are the results of the review valid?
- What are the results?
- Will the results help locally?

The 10 questions on the following pages are designed to help you think about these issues systematically. The first two questions are screening questions and can be answered quickly. If the answer to both is "yes," it is worth proceeding with the remaining questions. There is some degree of overlap between the questions, and you are asked to record a "yes," "no" or "can't tell" to most of the questions. A number of prompts are given after each question. These are designed to remind you why the question is important. Record your reasons for your answers in the spaces provided.

questions commonly appear in many other assessment tools. Nonetheless, the level of clarity embedded in each criterion must be noted here. Included are clear quality indicators that are also connected to the aforementioned aims of the research. Quality indicators such as *Appropriate, Address, Adequately, Take into consideration, Sufficiently, Clear*, and *Valuable* are well thought out in highlighting what is good enough.

The long version of CASP is shown in Box 3.5.

Here, I discuss two of the CASP criteria and further explore their subcriteria. Criterion 5 is about data collection and includes seven subcriteria. The focus of these seven subcriteria is convergent with *justification* in terms of (1) setting, (2) data collection process, (3) method, (4) use of the methods, (5) modified methods, (6) the forms of data, and (7) saturation of data. Criterion 8 concerns whether or not the data analysis is sufficiently rigorous. The major area of concern among the following six subcriteria is validity, which refers to a relationship between intent and cases. For example, data analysis in this review guideline is checked by a notion of validity in terms of selection of the data from the original sample; degree of sufficient data presented; ways of dealing with contradictory data; and critical examination of researcher's role, potential bias, and influence.

Cultural Anthropology (Timothy Elfenbein, PhD, personal communication, July 14, 2014)

This review guideline (Box 3.6) involves 10 criteria that cover key aspects of cultural anthropology from a broader perspective. By "broader perspective," it is meant that most of these evaluative criteria consist of broader or open-ended question forms. In addition, the editors of this journal provide reviewers with a broad direction of what to do rather than requiring them to mark points in a form of assessment rubric or to write comments in a certain way.

Table 3.5

CASP (Critical Appraisal Skills Programme, Headings) by the University of Oxford

1. Was there a clear statement of the aims of the research?	☐ Yes	☐ Can't tell	☐ No
2. Is a qualitative methodology appropriate?	☐ Yes	☐ Can't tell	☐ No
Is it worth continuing?			
3. Was the research design appropriate to address the aims of the research?	☐ Yes	☐ Can't tell	☐ No
4. Was the recruitment strategy appropriate to the aims of the research?	☐ Yes	☐ Can't tell	☐ No
5. Was the data collected in a way that addressed the research issue?	☐ Yes	☐ Can't tell	☐ No
6. Has the relationship between researcher and participants been adequately considered?	☐ Yes	☐ Can't tell	☐ No
7. Have ethical issues been taken into consideration?	☐ Yes	☐ Can't tell	☐ No
8. Was the data analysis sufficiently rigorous?	☐ Yes	☐ Can't tell	☐ No
9. Is there a clear statement of findings?	☐ Yes	☐ Can't tell	☐ No
10. How valuable is the research?	☐ Yes	☐ Can't tell	☐ No

Box 3.5. CASP (Critical Appraisal Skills Programme, Full Version)

....

Screening Questions

1. Was there a clear statement of the aims of the research?

HINT: Consider

- What was the goal of the research?
- Why it was thought important?
- Its relevance

☐ Yes   ☐ Can't tell   ☐ No

2. Is a qualitative methodology appropriate?

HINT: Consider

- If the research seeks to interpret or illuminate the actions and/or subjective experiences of research participants

Is qualitative research the right methodology for addressing the research goal?

☐ Yes   ☐ Can't tell   ☐ No

⇨ *Is it worth continuing?*

Detailed Questions

3. Was the research design appropriate to address the aims of the research?

HINT: Consider

- If the researcher has justified the research design (e.g. have they discussed how they decided which method to use?)

☐ Yes   ☐ Can't tell   ☐ No

4. **Was the recruitment strategy appropriate to the aims of the research?**   □ Yes   □ Can't tell   □ No

HINT: Consider

- If the researcher has explained how the participants were selected
- If they explained why the participants they selected were the most appropriate to provide access to the type of knowledge sought by the study
- If there are any discussions around recruitment (e.g. why some people chose not to take part)

5. **Was the data collected in a way that addressed the research issue?**   □ Yes   □ Can't tell   □ No

HINT: Consider

- If the setting for data collection was justified
- If it is clear how data were collected (e.g. focus group, semi-structured interview, etc.)
- If the researcher has justified the methods chosen
- If the researcher has made the methods explicit (e.g. for interview method, is there an indication of how interviews were conducted, or did they use a topic guide?)
- If methods were modified during the study. If so, has the researcher explained how and why?
- If the form of data is clear (e.g. tape recordings, video material, notes, etc.)
- If the researcher has discussed saturation of data

6. **Has the relationship between researcher and participants been adequately considered?**   □ Yes   □ Can't tell   □ No

HINT: Consider

- If the researcher critically examined their own role, potential bias and influence during
  (a) Formulation of the research questions
  (b) Data collection, including sample recruitment and choice of location
- How the researcher responded to events during the study and whether they considered the implications of any changes in the research design

7. **Have ethical issues been taken into consideration?**   □ Yes   □ Can't tell   □ No

HINT: Consider

- If there are sufficient details of how the research was explained to participants for the reader to assess whether ethical standards were maintained
- If the researcher has discussed issues raised by the study (e.g. issues around informed consent or confidentiality or how they have handled the effects of the study on the participants during and after the study)
- If approval has been sought from the ethics committee

8. **Was the data analysis sufficiently rigorous?**   □ Yes   □ Can't tell   □No

HINT: Consider

- If there is an in-depth description of the analysis process
- If thematic analysis is used. If so, is it clear how the categories/themes were derived from the data?
- Whether the researcher explains how the data presented were selected from the original sample to demonstrate the analysis process

- If sufficient data are presented to support the findings
- To what extent contradictory data are taken into account
- Whether the researcher critically examined their own role, potential bias and influence during analysis and selection of data for presentation

9. Is there a clear statement of findings?

☐ Yes   ☐ Can't tell   ☐ No

HINT: Consider

- If the findings are explicit
- If there is adequate discussion of the evidence both for and against the researchers' arguments
- If the researcher has discussed the credibility of their findings (e.g. triangulation, respondent validation, more than one analyst)
- If the findings are discussed in relation to the original research question

10. How valuable is the research?

HINT: Consider

- If the researcher discusses the contribution the study makes to existing knowledge or understanding (e.g. do they consider the findings in relation to current practice or policy?, or relevant research-based literature?)
- If they identify new areas where research is necessary
- If the researchers have discussed whether or how the findings can be transferred to other populations or considered other ways the research may be used

The guideline is so open-ended that reviewers of this journal are reminded to address as many questions as possible. In turn, this means that reviewers could address these questions as little as possible, depending on the nature and type of manuscripts they are reviewing. In doing so, this review guideline does not use language

Box 3.6. *Cultural Anthropology's* Review Guide

....

For Reviewers

Articles appropriate for the journal will differ stylistically, topically, and theoretically, but all should make a scholarly contribution of the highest caliber. In a cover email or letter, please assign the manuscript to one of the following categories: accept with minor revisions; revise and resubmit; reject. In the body of your review, please address as many of the following questions as are relevant to the article you are reviewing:

- Is the essay empirically rich?

- Is the essay richly contextualized, describing, for example, political-economic, techno-scientific, and demographic dynamics critical to its topic?

- Does the essay use empirical material to enhance theoretical insight?

- Are theoretical frameworks sound and clearly articulated?

- Does the essay make a novel theoretical contribution?

- Does the essay address topics of particular timely relevance?

- Does the essay illustrate or otherwise contribute to innovations in research design?

- Is the essay textually innovative?

- Does the writing meet a high standard of clarity, elegance, and/or compellingness?

- What communities of people (both within and beyond anthropology) are likely to be engaged by this essay?

or keywords encountered in conventional evaluation tools, such as *Research purpose and questions, Data collection, Data analysis and interpretation*, and *Results*. It is strongly believed that the characteristics inherent in this review guideline are in line with the nature of cultural anthropology that requires cultural anthropologists to not carry out certain expected research acts but also to make their fieldwork and products adaptive and innovative. I group the 10 open-ended criteria into the following five quality categories:

1. Richness of empirical data/contextualization
2. Theoretical framework/contribution
3. Timing/relevance
4. Innovative design/writing
5. Impact on audience

In summary, the positive aspects of this review guideline in the context of cultural anthropology are twofold: data-based rich description and innovation. It is likely that the editors of this journal value both tradition and change in a way that makes a newer synthesis of the field possible.

Journal of Organizational Ethnography

Major aims and scope of this relatively recently established qualitative research journal are as follows:

1) high-quality articles from original ethnographic research that contribute to the current and future development of qualitative intellectual knowledge and understanding of the nature of public and private sector work, organization and management; 2) articles examining the history and development of the contribution of ethnography to qualitative research in social, organization and management studies; and 3) articles examining the intellectual, pedagogical and practical use-value of ethnography in organization and management research, management education and management practice, or which extend, critique or challenge past and current theoretical and empirical knowledge claims within one or more of these areas of interest.

One of the three editors of this journal provided detailed procedures of how manuscripts are handled in the review processes:

Thank you for your e-mail. I was interested to hear about your research and many thanks for thinking about our journal. As you will be very aware that evaluation of qualitative research is a difficult task with little agreement on standard procedures and protocol for "objective" assessment. In terms of the *Journal of Organizational Ethnography* we require that papers are initially screened by one of three editors. If we think it has a chance of publication and is potentially of interest to our readers or would benefit from development we sent the paper out to anonymous peer review. We normally look for agreement between at least two if not all three reviewers before making a further decision. We chose our reviewers from our scholarly contacts including a well-developed conference network. Occasionally however we will need to search for someone not known to us specifically where we require subject or technical expertise. The reviewers are free to evaluate the paper however they want although we stress the importance we place on "developmental" feedback even if the decision is to reject the paper. We provide a template for reviewers (this is the closest we have to a rubric) but I must stress that it is NOT required for reviewers to use this.

—Matthew J. Brannan, PhD (personal communication,
July 14, 2014)

The way in which the editor of this journal illustrated its review process is logical, transparent, and supportive. It is logical because a submitted manuscript is reviewed at various levels. It is transparent because appropriate reviewers are actively identified. It is supportive because the word *development* is highlighted. Of course, many other qualitative journal editors utilize review policies and procedures similar to these. However, this journal appears to make them explicit (Box 3.7).

The six criteria of this review guideline are Originality, Relationship to literature, Methodology, Results, Practicality and/or research implications, and Quality of communication. It is worth noting that the fifth criterion, Practicality and/or research implications, stands out. In fact, although it is important to consider this aspect of qualitative research, authors often go to one extreme or the other. That is, authors either make large generalizations going

Box 3.7. *Journal of Organizational Ethnography's* Review Guide

1. **Originality**: Does the paper contain new and significant information adequate to justify publication?

2. **Relationship to literature**: Does the paper demonstrate an adequate understanding of the relevant literature in the field and cite an appropriate range of literature sources? Is any significant work ignored?

3. **Methodology**: Is the paper's argument built on an appropriate base of theory, concepts, or other ideas? Has the research or equivalent intellectual work on which the paper is based been well designed? Are the methods employed appropriate?

4. **Results**: Are results presented clearly and analyzed appropriately? Do the conclusions adequately tie together the other elements of the paper?

5. **Practicality and/or research implications**: Does the paper identify clearly any implications for practice and/or further research? Are these implications consistent with the findings and conclusions of the paper?

6. **Quality of communication**: Does the paper clearly express its case, measured against the technical language of the field and the expected knowledge of the journal's readership? Has attention been paid to the clarity of expression and readability, such as sentence structure, jargon use, acronyms, etc.?

beyond the scope of their findings or do not pay sufficient attention to this part of their research.

International Sociology

The aim and scope of *International Sociology* are as follows:

This peer-reviewed journal publishes contributions from diverse areas of sociology, with a focus on international and comparative approaches. The journal presents innovative theory and empirical approaches, with attention to insights into the sociological imagination that deserve worldwide attention. New ways of interpreting the social world and sociology from an international perspective provide innovative insights into key sociological issues.

As shown in Box 3.8, there are eight criteria for which reviewers are asked to rate on a scale of 1 through 5. Similar to some other review guidelines, this guideline first asks about essential aspects of the manuscript, such as *Importance, Topical relevance,* and *Originality,* which are three of the eight criteria. Interestingly, the next two criteria in this review guideline refer to something that is hardly encountered in other guidelines. The unique terms used in this guideline are *Argument* and *Strength of argumentation*; perhaps the word "argument" represents this journal's spirit. As seen in the aforementioned aim and scope, this journal looks for

Box 3.8. *International Sociology's* Review Guide

Please use a scale from 1–5 to indicate your evaluation of the paper on each of the criteria below.
1. Importance of the subject for *International Sociology's* field of interest
2. Topical relevance
3. Originality of approach
4. Argument is grounded in theoretical literature
5. Strength of argumentation and presentation of hypotheses
6. Quality of methodology and use of data (if applicable)
7. Presentation of analysis and findings (e.g., tables, symbols, and figures)
8. Quality and conciseness of writing
    Recommendation: _____ Accept
    _____ Minor Revision
    _____ Major Revision
    _____ Reject
    Would you be willing to review a revision of this manuscript?

Comments:

specific qualities and fresh insights deeply grounded in *sociological imagination, new ways of interpreting the social world*, or *innovative insights*.

Equity & Excellence in Education

The disciplinary area of this research journal is multicultural education. The review guideline is very simple but seems to cover essential qualities as much as possible (Box 3.9).

Three key elements of this review guideline are *Content, Organization*, and *Usefulness to readers*. It is rare for the third element, *Usefulness to readers*, to appear in review guidelines. Because the purpose of multicultural education is to make a change in policy and practice, considering the importance of the usefulness to the reader makes sense. Let me examine the other two broad criteria. The characteristics of *Content* are measured by three quality indicators—*Accuracy, Relevance*, and *Adequate research base*—which are commonly encountered in other review guidelines. Research itself must be accurate, relevant, and adequate in a way that expresses meaningful conclusions to the reader. Importantly, the subcriteria of *Content* are *Good fit* and the *Completeness argument*. The *Good fit* criterion is related to the mission of this journal, whereas *Completeness of argument* points out details of what is expected of the manuscript. That is, the reviewer is asked to assess qualities relative to *an adequate conceptual framework and a recent, comprehensive literature review*. As noted in Chapter 2, this kind of rubric dealing with applied fields of study is very thematic and open compared to those in traditionally known disciplinary fields, such as ethnography and phenomenology. The second criterion is about *Organization, Format*, and *Clarity*, which are measured by indicators such as *Being clear, Accessible*, and *Specific*.

Journal of Ethnographic and Qualitative Research

The *Journal of Ethnographic and Qualitative Research* (*JEQR*; Michael Firmin, PhD, personal communication, July 10, 2014) utilizes a review guideline that is very comprehensive and in-depth. As shown in (Table 3.6), it entails both a set of evaluative criteria and a set of open-ended questions. Here, I discuss the rubric of *JEQR*. There are 11 criteria in this rubric, and very interestingly, the first 3 criteria draw attention to an overall quality of the

Box 3.9. *Equity & Excellence in Education*'s Review Guide

CONTENT (Accuracy, Relevance, Adequate Research Base):

Please consider if the topic is a **good fit** with the journal's mission. Does it take a social justice perspective (dealing with the intersection of two or more social identities; examination of systemic implications)?

Comment on the **completeness of the argument** (provides an adequate conceptual framework; and provides a recent, comprehensive literature review so that the reader can track the development of the research thread for her/his own purposes)

> *For example, This paper is rich in the qualitative material it presents and the arguments flow well; however, the reader is NOT given any indication of the author's research methods, of who the participants were, how the study proceeded, etc. This is necessary for context and a fuller understanding of the project.*

ORGANIZATION, FORMAT, and CLARITY:

Does the manuscript flow from the framework to the data to the argument? Are the steps well connected? Clarity of the writing (clear, accessible, and specific?)

USEFULNESS TO READERS:

Rating:

____ **Accept** [Requires no revisions on the part of the author(s) and only minor copyediting by the editorial staff]

____ **Accept** [Use this category to indicate that you are suggesting revisions that you feel confident the author(s) can carry out.]

____ **Revise and resubmit** [Manuscript is of interest; it is something that would like to see published by *EEE*, requires major revisions (updated or enlarged literature review, shifts in argument, additional theoretical or analytical consideration, reorganization, etc.). Since we cannot be confident that author(s) may be willing or able to make the necessary changes, the editorial staff will need to see a revision prior to making a publication decision. *EEE* staff will assess a resubmission on the basis of your recommendations. Please be as specific as possible.

____ **Reject** [This manuscript does not seem suitable for publication in *EEE* as it has significant flaws. Please note that we like to provide useful feedback even when we reject a manuscript.]

manuscript. To my knowledge, there are no other rubrics in EQR that place an overall rate upfront. Typically, there is general agreement that this kind of summative assessment is placed at the end of scoring guides. Placing this overall judgmental criterion at the beginning of the rubric may serve just as meaningfully as placing it at the end. In fact, this kind of deductive approach to an assessment rubric is considered to be strengthened by the inclusion of two other criteria that particularly highlight the specific nature of ethnography and qualitative research—*writing form* and *APA style*. Perhaps reviewers may find their task easy because they are asked to answer a clear judgmental call first and to assess levels of effective written communication as well as the functional aspects of the manuscript.

After rating the three overall judgmental assessments, reviewers encountered the following major questions about the relationship between theory and practice: How to contextualize a problem? How did theory guide practice? or How did practice guide theory? These kinds of questions are relevant in assessing a key idea of how research was formulated, developed, and concluded in a way that helps the reader better understand a phenomenon under investigation. This holistic criterion, under Literature Review in this rubric, is regarded as appropriate in terms of what makes ethnographic/qualitative research ethnographic/qualitative from a historical, epistemological, theoretical perspective. Then, this review guideline proceeds in a typical order of research from criteria 5 to 11, which concern participants, methods, analysis, findings, discussions, and limitation and future research. The most unique aspect of this rubric is that there are two criteria on participants—the number of participants and appropriate participants. That is, reviewers are asked to evaluate if the author of the manuscript provided not only a rationale for the number of participants but also a direct relationship between problems being investigated and the characteristics of participants. Again, both criteria on participants can be combined into one criterion, but *JEQR* places great emphasis on the importance of why the number of participants who are selected and how research problems are actually answered by participants selected.

Following this evaluation rubric, *JEQR* presents the following open-ended statements for reviewers to complete. Although the final two open-ended statements are seen in other previously discussed guidelines, the language of this *JEQR* rubric is unique:

Table 3.6
Journal of Ethnographic and Qualitative Research's Review Guide

	Excellent	Good	Fair	Poor	Additional Comments (Optional)
1. **Overall quality/assessment**					
2. **Writing form** (e.g., active voice; sentence structure, "flow" from one section to the next)					
3. **Overall adherence to APA style and standards**					
4. **Literature review** (Does this author provide a thorough and clear review that sets up the problem that she/he explored? Does the author include relevant/recent citations? Does the author end the literature review explaining how his/her research adds to or complements existent scholarship? Overall, does the reader fully understand how the literature informed the author's research and vice versa?)					
5. **Number of participants** (Does the author provide or give an implied rationale for the number of participants she/he selected? To what extent does the number of participants give credibility to the author's overall findings?)					

6. **Appropriate participants** (Do you consider the type and number of participants adequate enough to address the problem that the author identified, as well as the interpretation provided?)						
7. **Description of method** (Does the author adequately describe how qualitative method *applied* to his/her study? That is, does the author explain how and why she/he used certain qualitative activities, as discussed in the research literature?)						
8. **Description of analysis** (Does the author provide a discussion about how she/he analyzed data and the rationale for his/her decisions?)						
9. **Findings** (Does the author weave participants' quotes and create a "story" that addresses the problem explored? That is, are quotes *incorporated* into the narrative versus being inserted at random?)						
10. **Discussion** (Does the author revisit the literature review and then discuss how the study's findings complement, add to, and/or contradict it?)						
11. **Limitation and future research** (Does the author cite his/her own shortcomings in the study and offer recommendations for future scholarship?)						

- Please state your overall impression of the rigor associated with this manuscript:
- Please describe perceived strengths of the manuscript:
- Please describe perceived weaknesses of the manuscript:
- Identify any revisions you think are necessary prior to publication:
- Please share any other information you think would help us make a decision about this manuscript:

The language used, such as "overall impressions of the rigor" and "strengths" and "weaknesses" of the manuscript, is not encountered in any of the previously discussed review guidelines. Taken together, it is certain that one of the major characteristics of ethnography is *empirical richness* or *in-depth exploration*. To meet this expectation, the fact that *JEQR* places great emphasis on inquiring into the credibility and appropriateness of participants is very reasonable. At the end of the rubric are five decision rules. Each decision includes specific instructions and explanations related to statuses. Decision 4 is similar to "accept with major revisions," but it does not use the word "accept." Instead, it is more an invitation to resubmit the manuscript without a certain promise. The five decision rules are as follows:

1. Publish: The manuscript is near flawless.
2. Publish pending a few slight matters that need to be addressed, as indicated in this review:
3. Offer the authors(s) an opportunity to revise and resubmit the manuscript, as strong potential for this manuscript is evident pending some revisions:
4. Offer the author(s) an opportunity to provide substantial revision and resubmission of this manuscript; the likelihood of publication potential is unclear based on the current version of the manuscript. As mentioned earlier, there have to be stories to be told and actual examples of interview questions that were asked to get those stories:
5. Reject the manuscript: The quality, rigor, content, and/or writing style do not meet the journal's standards; the errors are too many to warrant a revise/resubmission offer:

Grounded Theory Review: An International Journal

This review guideline (Astrid Gynnild, PhD, personal communication, July 26, 2014) (Box 3.10), just like any other, includes different kinds of decisions—for example, accept as it is, accept pending minor revisions, revise and resubmit, and reject.

Also, it has separate comments for authors and editors. At a glance, this grounded theory review journal is unique in that what is expected in this journal is comprehensive in nature. In other words, criteria such as a clearer focus or composition are general characteristics of any research, whereas the rest of the criteria are directly related to specific characteristics of grounded theory. In particular, more attention is paid to grounded theory-related criteria such as "core category," "theoretical propositions," and "brief statement on data collection & analysis needs to be consistent with classic GT methodology."

Box 3.10. The *Grounded Theory Review: An International Journal's* Review Guide

Basis for Revision

- Needs a clearer focus ☐
- Core category needs clarification ☐
- Related concepts need clarification ☐
- Theoretical propositions (hypotheses) need
  to be clearly articulated ☐
- Contribution to knowledge (addressing
  the literature) needs further work ☐
- Implications for practice need to be addressed ☐
- Limitations of the study need to be addressed ☐
- Data sources need to be addressed ☐
- Brief statement on data collection & analysis
  needs to be consistent with classic GT methodology ☐
- Composition needs work ☐
- Other (provide comments below)

Conclusion

This chapter explored three broad areas in which the evaluation of qualitative research is practically understood. The first area that was examined concerned AERA's "Standards for Reporting on Empirical Social Science Research". It is generally believed that AERA plays a key role in leading the educational research community. As such, AERA's "Standards" is considered to be a very influential research guideline not only for AERA-related research acts (annual conference proposals and other in-house journals, such as *Review of Educational Research* and *Review of Research in Education*) but also for many other research associations and/or journals. The two major criteria are warrantability and transparency. The second area that was explored in this chapter concerned recent scholarly discourses about reviewing a variety of qualitative research. Trainor and Graue's (2013) book, *Reviewing Qualitative Research in the Social Sciences*, is believed to be the first attempt to inquire into the issue of quality in qualitative research. They did not use the word "evaluation" but instead used the words "estimate or review." Furthermore, they did not intend to place their scholarly attempt in the context of research journals. Instead, they attempted to draw broad attention from the qualitative research community to the appropriate ways of reviewing all sorts of products done qualitatively. It is certain that the review touchstones proposed by scholars performing different kinds of qualitative research are worthwhile at this time. Last, this chapter examined the review guides of current qualitative research journals that consisted largely of two preferences—non-use and use of evaluation tools. Journal editors who do not provide reviewers specific evaluation tools are competent in obtaining the quality reviews they want, mainly because they strongly believe that not only does the non-use of review guidelines reflect a free and creative spirit of qualitative research but also the editors believe that select reviewers have the necessary expertise and professional conduct to provide them with quality reviews. These editors believe "the less, the better." On the other hand, a handful of research journals provide reviewers with specific evaluation tools in several different formats. Reviewers are asked to answer a series of broad and specific questions or to rate numeric values (1–5) or levels of quality (Excellent, Good, Fair, or Good) on evaluative rubrics. Reviewers can also be requested to provide specific comments in correspondence with the specific evaluative criteria. Regardless of which preferences or forms are chosen, reviewers are required to write qualitative comments and to offer a decision to be made from four typical choices: acceptance as is, acceptance with minor changes, acceptance with major changes, or rejection. Consequently, I conclude this chapter by reflecting on three possible ways of understanding the evaluation of qualitative research. First, the reader is reminded of the discussion in Chapter 2 regarding a holistic view of evaluation of qualitative research. My scholarly attempt in this book is to create a big picture of how the evaluative act of the manuscript (or even the dissertation or master's thesis draft) is holistically understood in an effort to constantly improve our perceptions and practicality pertaining to the quality of qualitative research. In this way, I believe we qualitative researchers can find collective wisdom useful for improving our research acts from within. To this end, Figure 3.1 presents a quadratic aspect of the evaluation of qualitative research.

To elaborate, this holistic view of the evaluation of qualitative research is twofold. First, it is likely for a community of researchers to hold core values or beliefs regarding ideal qualitative research processes and products. Second, the community has options to include criteria related to research processes (question, theory, literature, design, data collection and interpretation, results and discussions, and conclusion and implication) and/or to key dimensions (originality, innovation, creativity, participants, reflexivity, writing, etc.). Together, a community of researchers can make a choice from five possible developments in the consideration of the evaluation of qualitative research. There may be some overlap among the five developments, depending on certain criteria in the review policies and practices (Table 3.7).

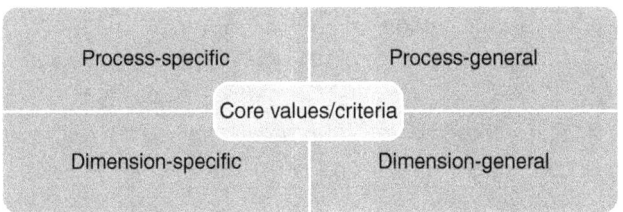

Figure 3.1 A Quadratic Aspect of EQR.

Next, I analyzed all specific evaluative tools of the 17 qualitative research journals mentioned in both Chapter 2 and Chapter 3 that included a variety of criteria for assessing the quality of manuscripts (Table 3.8).

Considering the seven most commonly used criteria, I found all of them meaningfully related to each other. Let me rearrange them as follows:

To elaborate, it is typical to think first about *a quality* such as "originality." Then, *the importance to the field* follows. The quality of *theoretical framework* should be strongly considered. As always, *the selection of participants* is important to reviewers because it is a determining factor for the sources of data. Those new to the field who seem to have no clear sense of *data analysis methods* usually criticize qualitative researchers. *Writing* is a fundamental aspect of research, and it is considered even more important in the field of

Qualities → Importance to the field → Theoretical framework → Participant → Data analysis → Writing → Impact/Readership

Table 3.7

Five Possible Developments in EQR

1. Use of core values/criteria only	Journals with no prescriptive criteria, *QSE: International Journal of Qualitative Studies in Education*
2. Core values/criteria with process-general criteria	*Action Research Journal, Qualitative Inquiries in Music Therapy, International Journal of Qualitative Methods, Journal of Organizational Ethnography*
3. Core values/criteria with process-specific criteria	*Narrative Inquiry in Bioethics,* SAGE's Reviewer Gateway, CASP, *Journal of Ethnographic and Qualitative Research*
4. Core values/criteria with dimension-general criteria	*International Sociology, Grounded Theory Review*
5. Core values/criteria with dimension-specific criteria	*Cultural Anthropology, Equity & Excellence in Education*

Table 3.8
Analysis of 17 Qualitative Research Journals' Review Guides

Code	Keywords
Paradigm (1)	Extent to which study exemplifies qualitative paradigm
Background (1)	Background/Study justification/Summary of pilot work
Originality (4)	Originality of approach (3); Worthy
Qualities (9)	Empirically rich; Overall quality; Organized and focused; Clear and comprehensive; Rich rigor (2); Focus (2); Meaningful coherence
Purpose/Problem/ Question (5)	A clear statement of the aims of the research; Clarity of purpose; Clear purpose and scope; Articulation of objectives (2)
Theoretical Framework (6)	Sound theoretical frameworks (2); Analytical; Perspective(s); Theoretical propositions (hypotheses) need to be clearly articulated; Related concepts need clarification
Literature Review (2)	Literature review; Relationship to literature
Design (2)	Innovative design; Appropriate research design to address the aims of the research
Context (3)	Richly contextualized; Credibility; Setting
Methodology (3)	Explanation and justification of method; Appropriate methodology; Quality of methodology and use of data (if applicable)
Participant (6)	Participants (2); Partnership and participation; Appropriateness of participant selection; Sampling/recruitment; Appropriate recruitment strategy
Data Sources (2)	Data sources; Data sources/evidence
Method (3)	Description of method; Methods and process (2)

(*continued*)

Table 3.8
Continued

Code	Keywords
Data Collection (3)	Data collection (3)
Data Analysis (7)	Description of analysis; Presentation of analysis and findings (e.g., tables, symbols, and figures); Data analysis (2); Data heading/analysis; Rigorous data analysis; Core category
Finding/Result (5)	Findings; Relevance of findings to data; A clear statement of findings; Results; Results/warrants for arguments
Discussion (2)	Discussion; Use empirical material to enhance theoretical insight
Argument (3)	Argument is grounded in theoretical literature; Strength of argumentation and presentation of hypotheses; Whether the argument is clear and logical/complete or flow of argument
Conclusion (2)	Conclusions valid; The conclusions presented are supported by the results or evidence presented
Writing (9)	Textually innovative; Writing has a high standard of clarity, elegance, and/or compellingness; Writing form overall adherence to APA style and standards; Clarity of writing; Reporting; Quality communication; Composition; Quality of written language; Overall communication of main points
Implication (3)	Actionability; Practicality and/or research implications; Implications for practice
Validity/Reliability	Whether the paper is internally consistent
Researcher (5)	Sincerity; Reflexivity; Personal characteristics; Relationship with participants (2)
Human subject (4)	Ethics (4)
Limitation (2)	Limitation and future research; Limitation

Table 3.8
Continued

Code	Keywords
Importance to the field (14)	Topics of particular timely relevance; Topical relevance; Importance of the subject; Significant contribution; Make a novel theoretical contribution; Significance of the study (5); Contribution to action research theory/practice; Contribution to knowledge; Relevancy to the publication; Valuable research
Impact/Readership (6)	What communities of people (both within and beyond anthropology) are likely to be engaged by this essay; Provocative content (new and thought-provoking); Interesting reading; Resonance; The accessibility of the paper to a broad readership; Usefulness to readers
Organization/ Structure (4)	Organization of report (2); Technical accuracy; Structure of the paper
Technicality (4)	Whether the title of the article is suitable or effective; Effectiveness of the article abstract and introduction; Whether the abstract is a good summary of the article; Accuracy of reference
Supplemental (1)	Full copies of interview schedules/Focus group schedule/Fieldwork plans

Note: ( ) for frequency.

The seven most commonly used evaluation criteria are as follows:

1. Importance to the field (14)
2. Qualities (9)
3. Writing (9)
4. Data Analysis (7)
5. Theoretical Framework (6), Participant (6), Impact/Readership (6)

qualitative research. *Impact/readership* is a deeper consideration of viewing the stakeholder and the reader as a part of qualitative research. In summary, these seven core criteria are those most commonly used in many contemporary qualitative research journals.

In addition, one needs to consider the purpose of the evaluation of qualitative research. In general, the evaluative act involves both judgment and learning. What has been explored and discussed thus far greatly has to do with judgment. It is obvious that the quality of the manuscript can be improved if the author is knowledgeable in advance about how it will be assessed. The fact is that the practice of qualitative research never actually unfolds in a linear way but, rather, in a very flexible way. Carlos Calderón Gómez (2009) wrote a seminal article titled "Assessing the Quality of Qualitative Health Research: Criteria, Process and Writing," which deals with both the methodological requirements and the substantive components of qualitative health research. Gómez views qualitative research practices as "a dynamic process in which quality has to be generated at each and every step of the research process" (p. 28). As such, the matter of quality in qualitative research that Gómez searches for in this assessment model is something a researcher can obtain through his or her ongoing, continuous, critical efforts throughout the research processes. Three dimensions—criteria, process, and writing—are visually presented in this model and are explained as connected and integrated. Thus, it is suggested that qualitative researchers deeply make sense of a notion of quality not by just following the external criteria that they see but, rather, by interconnecting these three dimensions with each other. That is, qualitative researchers actively attempt to unpack given criteria to the extent to which they can apply them to their actual research processes until generating actual texts. In summary, review guides should be integrated into research processes and products in a holistic way. Review guides, full of criteria, should serve as a self-regulated, pedagogical tool to internally generate the quality of qualitative research.

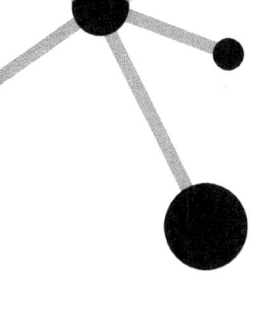

4

CHANGE, CHALLENGES, AND MIXED METHODS

The criteria for judging a good account have never been settled and are changing.

—Clifford (1986, p. 9)

Introduction

In recent years, discourse on whether or not it is possible to measure the value of qualitative research from the standpoint of conventional evaluation criteria has dramatically resurfaced. Those who accept a positivist paradigm argue more than ever that reality should be objectively measured. Advocates of this viewpoint are reigniting the paradigm wars in ways that repeat old arguments in new form. In fact, the new focus of the attack or criticism is on the shaky nature of evidence drawn from qualitative research. Fortunately, many leading qualitative scholars and researchers have made counterarguments at various levels. As has been explored in Chapters 2 and 3, approaches to the evaluation of qualitative research (EQR) and their review guides within the qualitative community have advanced in such a way that they will help guide future qualitative researchers to produce better quality products.

Those who are in the camp of mixed methods research are also more actively in search of a better validation process of research findings. In this chapter, I explore contemporary discourses on EQR in three areas: the evolution of the theoretical framework, the politics of evidence, and the evaluation of mixed methods.

The Changing Nature of Evaluative Criteria

In the previous two chapters, I described and explained the wide variety of approaches to EQR as well as provided examples through discussion of EQR approaches used by many different qualitative journals. Different approaches to EQR are linked to different epistemological underpinnings and are actualized by journal editors through a broad array of assessment strategies and instruments to evaluate manuscripts. Nonetheless, despite extant models and frameworks and the various ways of evaluating qualitative works that are available, we researchers are always faced with uncertainty and are working in dynamic, constantly changing contexts—socially, personally, and politically. As noted previously, there is, and always will be, a need to continue to examine emergent evaluation prescriptions and proposals and to juxtapose these with contemporary evolutions in context and culture. Richardson's evolving work on this topic provides a good example. Richardson (2000, p. 937) offers five criteria against which to assess the validity/quality of ethnographic texts:

- *Substantive contribution*: Does this piece contribute to our understanding of social-life? Does the writer demonstrate a deeply grounded (if embedded) human-world understanding and perspective? How has this perspective informed the construction of the text?
- *Aesthetic merit*: Does this piece succeed aesthetically? Does the use of creative analytical practices open up the text, invite interpretive responses? Is the text artistically shaped, satisfying, complex, and not boring?
- *Reflexivity*: How did the author come to write this text? How was the information gathered? Ethical issues? How has the author's subjectivity been both a producer and a product of this text? Is there adequate self-awareness and self-exposure for the reader to make judgments about the

point of view? Do authors hold themselves accountable to the standards of knowing and telling of the people they have studied?

- *Impact*: Does this affect me? Emotionally? Intellectually? Generate new questions? Move me to write? Move me to try to new research practices? Move me to action?
- *Express a reality*: Does this text embody a fleshed out, embodied sense of lived-experience? Does it seem "true"—a credible account of a cultural, social, individual, or communal sense of the "real"?

To my knowledge, the evaluative questions listed previously concerning ethnographic texts can be applied to judging most qualitative texts. As a journal referee, one must be concerned with a degree of contribution, a sense of aesthetics, the level of a researcher's reflection, the learning of the reader, and indications of credibility. It appears, however, that Richardson's criteria have changed. When writing in 2005, Richardson together with St. Pierre excluded the last criterion, *express a reality*. There is no explanation as to why this criterion is no longer included in the later version, even though there must have been a reason(s) behind their changed work.

As one journal editor mentioned, "Evaluation of qualitative research is a difficult task with little agreement on standard procedures and protocol for 'objective' assessment" (Matthew J. Brannan, personal communication, 2014). It is typical for research methodologists to offer a set of evaluative criteria that are claimed to be relevant and necessary based on their theoretical underpinnings. Many of the scholars and journal editors highlighted in previous chapters have done so, and these methodologies illustrate that some criteria are commonly used, whereas other criteria are used uniquely, depending on the different purposes and uses of the evaluation. However, by examining the matter of EQR from a broader perspective, I may end up claiming that EQR, just like other theoretical constructions in social science, is simultaneously contextual, cultural, and political. When a reviewer evaluates a manuscript, it is individualistic and difficult to describe the multiple influences impacting the reviewer's perspective. These individualistic and hidden meanings used by a reviewer do not necessarily neatly match the set of criteria provided by a journal editor, colleague, or conference organizer. Assessment tools in this complex process are used for formality, convenience, and as a standardized means to ensure fairness in determining who will be contributors. In the end, it is the reviewer's construction of meaning around the text (or lack thereof) that matters.

By the same token, an inclusion or exclusion of goodness criterion is socially constructed. The previously noted discrepancy between Richardson (2000) and Richardson and St. Pierre (2005) serves as an example. The omission must be more than random. The co-authors likely include the criteria that are agreed upon and co-constructed understandings, while omitting the one they do not. A consistent theme across both authors' individual and collaborative work is the joining of art and science in the production of qualitative texts: "Science is one lens, and creative art is another. We see more deeply using two lenses. I want to look through both lenses to see 'a social science art form'—a radically interpretive form of representation" (Richardson & St. Pierre, 2005, p. 964).

Perhaps, the qualitative research community accepts these scholars' social science art form, which is similar to what Lather (1986) refers to as "a new rigor of softness . . . validity of knowledge in process . . . an objective subjectivity" (p. 78). A social science art form or an objective subjectivity is something that continues to evolve. Many journal editors also express that their review guidelines go through constant revision processes. A constant deliberation on the inclusion and exclusion of criteria in EQR is necessary to better address the changing nature of knowledge and aesthetics in sociocultural contexts.

Politics of Evidence

Despite the evolution of robust evaluation frameworks, work remains on at least two fronts. Internally, as a community of qualitative researchers, we need to continue to focus on the purposes of our scholarly work and the ways we legitimize it both within and outside our fields. This, necessarily, is a never-ending conversation and one in which all researchers should participate. Externally, we need to continue to focus on appropriate responses to those that diminish the rigorously obtained knowledge that results from naturalistic inquiry. Those that prioritize only randomized, generalizable work with numerical findings (despite the inherent associated problems) ignore a robust knowledge base that, pedagogically, often has more to offer than a statistical analysis of decontextualized "data." This knowledge base presents in narrative form as stories, and as humans and inquirers, it is among our most basic ways of knowing (Riessman, 2008). Unfortunately, as mentioned previously, those who perpetuate paradigm wars also wield a great deal of power in research and policy communities.

As implied previously, current discourse on politics of evidence is mostly a resurrection of old-fashioned epistemological debates, which are initiated from several organizations or councils at the national level in the United States—for example, the National Research Council, the Society for Research on Educational Effectiveness, the Cochrane, the Campbell Methods Group, and What Works Clearinghouse. These trends are generally called scientifically based research (SBR) or the evidence-based movement (EBM). The extended discussion goes beyond the scope of this chapter. The main epistemological questions that need to be asked, just like 40 years ago, are "Whose science? Whose scientific principles?" (Denzin, 2009, p. 141). Related to the inquiry of this chapter, we ask, "Whose criteria?"

However, there are external forces that question not only quality in qualitative research but also its legitimacy. For example, mixed methods scholars and researchers try not to view themselves as postpositivists in the research paradigms that have been well established during the past several decades (Guba & Lincoln, 1994, 2000, 2005; Lincoln, Lynham, & Guba, 2011), but instead seek to create their own hybrid, pragmatic epistemology—one that is prioritized over qualitative research. The current neoconservative initiatives—the National Research Council or the Society for Research on Educational Effectiveness (Denzin, 2009; Denzin & Giardina, 2009)—diminish the tradition of qualitative inquiry that values *understanding* in human science by narrowly defining what research is and how it should be assessed. Denzin and Giardina (2009) point to the necessity of casting "big-tent" criteria to evaluate qualitative research in the context of a changing epistemological and political context:

> We must expand the size of our tent, indeed we need a bigger tent! We cannot afford to fight with one another. Mixed-methods scholars have carefully studied the many different branches of the poststructural tree. . . . The same cannot be

said for the poststructuralists. Nor can we allow the arguments from the SBR community to divide us. We must learn from the paradigm conflicts of the 1980s to not over-reach, to not engage in polemics, to not become too self-satisfied. We need to develop and work with our own concepts of science, knowledge, and quality inquiry. We need to remind the resurgent postpositivists that their criterion of good work applies only to work within their paradigm, not ours. (pp. 32–33)

Nonetheless, some prestigious qualitative journals do not provide these kinds of criteria or guidelines for their reviewers. Instead, reviewers invited by these journals are provided very general guidelines. For example, *QSE: International Journal of Qualitative Studies in Education* has no specific criteria to be used in reviewing manuscripts. Nonetheless, editorial manager Elsa Gonzalez (personal communication, August 16, 2012) has confidence in this open process:

Reviewers are free to send any comment to the author. We have very strong scholars to agree to review and most of the time, our reviewers are very detailed (without asking them) in their reviews from grammar, to format, to content . . . many of them go and make comments to each section of the manuscript (intro, methodology, results, conclusions).

This confidence and trust are also evident in many other prestigious qualitative journals that do not have specific review forms. Together, in this open-ended review process, I find a sense of autonomy, fit, trust, and professional ethics. Reviewers who have expertise know what is worth assessing and how good is good enough.

As reviewed in Chapter 2, Tracy (2010) presents a proposal for a model to ensure EQR. Tracy's model is a solid synthesis of what has been researched and theorized about in recent history. Alternatively, Lichtman's (2006) review of EQR includes *personal criteria*, which are based on her philosophy and assumptions regarding a good piece of qualitative research. That is, Lichtman attempts to make her personal philosophy explicit by reflecting on the self, the other, and interaction of the self/other. Lichtman argues that "an understanding of the other does not come about without an understanding of the self and how the self and other connect" (p. 192). She goes on to state, "I believe each is transformed through this research process" (p. 192). In contrast, Tracy (2010) takes an objective stance in establishing her model's rationale for education establishment *power holders*:

> In addition to providing a parsimonious pedagogical tool, I hope my conceptualization may aid in garnering respect for qualitative methods from power holders who know little about our work. Despite the gains of qualitative research in the late 20th century, a methodological conservatism has crept upon social science over the last 10 years . . . evidenced in governmental and funding agencies' preference for research that is quantitative, experimental, and statistically generalizable. . . . High ranking decision makers—in powerful governmental, funding, and institutional review board positions—are often unprepared and unable to appropriately evaluate qualitative analyses that feature ethnography, case study, and naturalistic data. (pp. 837–838)

With these pedagogical and political purposes in mind, Tracy (2010) provides eight *universal* hallmarks for high-quality qualitative methods across paradigms, suggesting that each criterion of quality can be approached via a variety of paths and crafts, the combination of which depends on the specific researcher, context, theoretical affiliation, and project. Tracy's eight "big-tent" criteria and *QSE's* simple scholarly decision recommendation with open-ended comments are two extreme approaches within the qualitative research community. Those situated in the positivist epistemology and mixed methods scholars will likely prefer Tracy's "big-tent" criteria for EQR over *QSE's* simple form. This is not because Tracy's reconstruction of other scholars' constructs is absolutely truthful or valid in itself but, rather, because Tracy's approach is procedural in terms of a logical flow of what a reviewer needs to do. The advantage of the "big-tent" procedural criteria is that they are in line with being normative to the extent to which a reviewer should not disregard the work of an author due to a disagreement with the author's epistemology. This also applies at the other extreme—*QSE's* recommendation sheet with open-ended comments, on which a reviewer has the freedom to make a scholarly judgment. The current debate on the politics of evidence is too heavy on ideology while giving too little attention to ethical concerns. It is time to think seriously about Donmoyer's (2012) article, "Can Qualitative Researchers Answer Policy-Makers' Simple 'What Works' Question?" which is not a new but, rather, recurring question the qualitative research community must collectively prepare to answer *again* and *well*.

Evaluation of Mixed Methods

Mixed methods research is gaining more attention than ever before from many disciplinary areas. Several attempts have been made to identify evaluative criteria for assessing the quality of mixed method research. Sale and Brazil's (2004) seminal article, "A Strategy to Identify Critical Appraisal Criteria for Primary Mixed-Method Studies," is an example. Heyvaert, Hannes, Maes, and Onghena (2013) select 13 articles that include evaluation criteria or frameworks and identify the following three groups of criteria:

1. Specific critical appraisal criteria for the qualitative and quantitative stands of a mixed methods research study
2. Specific critical appraisal criteria for mixed methods research
3. Generic critical appraisal criteria

While reviewing all three groups of criteria in detail, Heyvaert et al. (2013) endorse the second group of criteria that adopts "a critical appraisal instrument specifically designed for mixed methods research studies" (p. 317). The *Journal of Mixed Method Research* (*JMMR*), first published in 2007, is widely known and circulated. Donna Mertens (2013), one of the editors of this journal, shares her own scholarly view of how to review mixed methods manuscripts in Trainor and Graue's (2013) book, *Reviewing Qualitative Research in the Social Sciences*. Her six touchstones are as follows:

1. The researcher makes clear the assumptions that provide the philosophical frame for the research by providing explicit explanations of the axiological, epistemological, ontological, and methodological assumptions.

2. Researchers should be explicit about the theoretical frameworks that inform their work and how the frameworks influence the research process and findings.
3. Researchers should make explicit their mixed methods design, including the design of both quantitative and qualitative parts of the study and the points of intersection.
4. Mixed methods research involves having samples for both qualitative and quantitative portions of the study; hence, researchers need to clarify their rationale for the samples selected, the methods they used for the different samples, and the implications of the similarities and differences between the samples.
5. Data collection procedures need to be explained for both quantitative and qualitative portions of the study; adherence to quality in data collection needs to be demonstrated for each type of data.
6. Data analysis in mixed methods studies should adhere to standards for quality for analysis of both quantitative and qualitative data, tensions between the outcomes of the different analyses must be addressed, and inferences should be clearly linked with the data analysis.

Mertens (2013) is concerned with philosophical frame, theoretical framework, design/the points of intersection, rationale for samples and methods, data collection procedures, and data analysis—all of which must be well balanced in both qualitative and quantitative portions of the study. As is known, advocates of mixed methods research adopt a pragmatic philosophy that seeks practical solutions. Given the nature of this field of study, mixed methods researchers must present a paradigmatic discourse that explains characteristics of the value, knowledge, reality, and method adopted. Therefore, it makes sense that this review guideline places four assumptions underpinning a nature of paradigm upfront. The remaining five touchstones follow what are encountered in a typical research paper—that is, theoretical framework, design, sample, data collection, and data analysis.

Leech, Dellinger, Brannagan, and Tanaka (2010) attempt to identify how to evaluate the quality of mixed methods research. They reviewed literature to identify what existing criteria are available to measure the quality of mixed methods research. They examine four points to evaluate mixed methods research by Creswell and Clark (2007) and summarize them as follows:

> (a) Determining if the study is a mixed research study; (b) deciding whether rigorous mixed methods are used; (c) identifying the mixed research purpose statement, research question, type of mixed method design, and data analyses; and (d) establishing whether the study's author(s) present information regarding challenges that may have arisen during the study (e.g., unequal sample sizes, how participants were selected, the steps taken throughout the study). (p. 18)

Leech et al. (2010, p. 19) assess that the four points to evaluate mixed methods research and other existing review criteria are too broad to apply in the review process. Instead, they propose the validation framework that consists of the following five elements:

1. The foundational element
2. The elements of construct validation for quantitative, qualitative, and mixed research
3. Inferential consistency
4. The utilization/historical element
5. The consequential element

To elaborate, the reviewer first examines a foundation on which the article stands—a foundation that includes a variety of constructs pertaining to idea formulation and purpose statement in light of the review of literature. Second, the reviewer pays great attention to methodological constructs relative to design, legitimation (samples, weakness, sequence, or commensurability), and rigor (interpretation or integration) in reference with qualitative and quantitative research. The reviewer then assesses a way in which theory, purpose, literature, and measurement are appropriately linked and meaningfully inferred from one another. The fourth and fifth elements that the reviewer investigates are how the results would possibly be utilized and what consequences are presumed to occur, respectively. Together, this validation framework used to evaluate the quality of mixed methods research follows a typical process of research, from purpose/question to literature review, design, analysis/interpretation, results, and conclusion/ impact. What is unique about this validation framework, however, is that Leech et al. regard these typical research processes as a set of constructs that need to be described, explained, and justified, both logically and pragmatically. Furthermore, the effort made by these scholars to perform a comprehensive review of the literature of qualitative research regarding validity, criteria, or techniques is admirable.

It is useful for readers to review a list of terms associated with the evaluation of qualitative research noted by mixed methods researchers. In the validation framework, there are three boxes that deal with methodological constructs, with a box of mixed methods being located in the middle between the other quantitative and qualitative boxes. Box 4.1 is a qualitative box in which a glossary of evaluation terms is provided. The only concern that needs to be addressed is that all these key evaluative terms and techniques in the field of qualitative research must be treated as a whole. In other words, the essential nature of qualitative research is subtly represented by criteria such as uniqueness, distinctiveness, particularity, depth, sensitivity, human politics, collaboration, power, reflexivity, humility, and social justice. I believe that mixed methods researchers treat qualitative research in a somewhat rough and technical manner in that they appear to regard diverse, complex, proliferated, contested, and evolving fields of qualitative research as a unitary field of study.

Here, I discuss this issue using the *Journal of Mixed Methods Research* (*JMMR*) as an example. The following is an excerpt of the aims and the scope of *JMMR* (http://www.sagepub.com/journals/ Journal201775):

> The journal's scope includes exploring a global terminology and nomenclature for mixed methods research, delineating where mixed methods research may be used most effectively, creating the paradigmatic and philosophical foundations for mixed methods research, illuminating design and procedure issues, and determining the logistics of conducting mixed methods research.

Very importantly, *JMMR* openly presents its review criteria for the manuscripts submitted (http://www.sagepub.com/journals/Journ al201775#tabview=manuscriptSubmission). Two different review

Box 4.1. Traditional Qualitative Elements of Construct Validation Within Mixed Methods Research

Traditional Qualitative Elements of Construct Validation

Primary criteria	Secondary criteria
Credibility	Explicitness
Authenticity	Vividness
Criticality	Creativity
Integrity	Thoroughness
Congruence	
Sensitivity	
Other terms used	
Transferability	Descriptive validity
Consistency	Interpretive validity
Reference adequacy	Theoretical validity
Triangulation	Evaluative validity
Crystallization	Generalizability
Structural relationships	Auditability
Explanation credibility	Confirmability

Different Types of Techniques for Design, Considerations, Data Gathering, Analysis, and Presentation

Giving voice, Persistent observation, Peer debriefing, Dependability audit, Triangulation, Articulating decisions, Reflective journaling, Member checking

Source: Leech et al. (2010).

criteria are available—one for empirical research and the other for methodological/theoretical discussions (Box 4.2).

The 11 review criteria listed in Box 4.2 include both general and specific elements of what constitutes good research. The first criterion, Noteworthiness of the problem, is an overarching quality indicator similar to criteria such as Originality, Novelty, Creativity,

Box 4.2. *Journal of Mixed Methods Research*'s Review Guide on Empirical Research

The review criteria for **empirical research** include:

- Noteworthiness of the problem
- Theoretical framework
- Fit of questions to mixed methods design
- Mixed methods design
- Mixed methods sampling
- Mixed methods analysis and integration
- Insightfulness of discussion
- Writing quality
- Quality of conclusions
- Contribution to mixed methods literature
- Interest to *JMMR* readership

and Innovation. The remaining 10 criteria are in correspondence with a typical form of research.

Box 4.3 presents *JMMR*'s review criteria for conceptual papers. Seven criteria measure the quality of mixed method research papers on methodological and theoretical discussions. They are very concise, and most are similar in nature. The three criteria that are different from the aforementioned review criteria on empirical research are Adequacy of the literature, Soundness of the

Box 4.3. *Journal of Mixed Methods Research*'s Review Guide on Methodological/Theoretical Discussions

The review criteria for **methodological/theoretical discussions** include:

- Addresses an important topic
- Adequacy of the literature
- Soundness of the argument
- Originality of the suggestions
- Writing quality
- Contribution to mixed methods literature
- Interest to *JMMR* readership

argument, and Originality of suggestion. In particular, attention needs to be paid to Soundness of the argument and Originality of suggestion, both of which are uniquely stated in expecting sound argument and original suggestions from the author of the manuscript. Although such criteria as soundness and originality are occasionally mentioned in review guidelines, it is rare for both criteria to be used back to back in reference to arguments and suggestions.

Comparing Review Criteria Between Qualitative and Mixed Methods Journals

Due to different disciplinary traditions and knowledge bases, it may be difficult to compare review criteria between qualitative and mixed methods journals. Nonetheless, it is possible to identity some common core qualities underlying different fields of study, which may provide the qualitative research community with a broad perspective on what good qualitative research entails. Table 4.1 compares the empirical research review guide with three qualitative review guides to identify similarities and differences pertaining to quality. As can be seen in the table, it appears that there are more differences than similarities across the five columns. The first column presents review criteria derived in 1987 as a classic viewpoint of how to evaluate qualitative research (which can even be applicable for quantitative research). The second column presents criteria of the *Journal of Mixed Methods Research*, followed by criteria of *Cultural Anthropology, Journal of Ethnographic and Qualitative Research*, and *International Sociology*, respectively.

I selected these last three journals for the purpose of comparing them with *JMMR*. These three journals were purposely selected because they are grounded in anthropology, ethnography, and sociology, which have different review criteria specific to their manuscripts. I derived the following conclusions from analyzing Table 4.1:

- The general evaluative criteria of 1987 still serve as a basic platform.
- Four core areas of these review criteria are Originality, Process, Writing, and Impact.

Table 4.1
Comparing Review Criteria Between Mixed Methods and Qualitative Research

General Evaluative Criteria (Cobb & Hagemaster, 1987)	*Journal of Mixed Methods Research*	*Cultural Anthropology*	*Journal of Ethnographic and Qualitative Research*	*International Sociology*
Expertise				
Purpose	Noteworthiness of the problem			Originality of approach
Problem and/or research question	Fit of questions to mixed methods design	Empirically rich?	Overall quality	
	Theoretical framework	Sound theoretical frameworks?		
Literature review			Literature review	
	Mixed methods design	Innovative design?		Quality of methodology and use of data (if applicable)
Context		Richly contextualized?		
Sample	Mixed methods sampling		Participants	
Data collection			Description of method	

(continued)

Table 4.1
Continued

General Evaluative Criteria (Cobb & Hagemaster, 1987)	Journal of Mixed Methods Research	Cultural Anthropology	Journal of Ethnographic and Qualitative Research	International Sociology
Data processing and plans for analysis	Mixed methods analysis and integration		Description of analysis	Presentation of analysis and findings (e.g., tables, symbols, and figures)
			Findings	
	Insightfulness of discussion		Discussion	Argument grounded in theoretical literature; strength of argumentation and presentation of hypotheses
	Writing quality	Textually innovative? Writing has high standard of clarity, elegance, and/or compellingness?	Writing form overall adherence to APA style and standards	Quality and conciseness of writing

Quality of conclusions		
Contribution to mixed methods literature	Use empirical material to enhance theoretical insight? Make a novel theoretical contribution?	
Human subject		
		Limitation and future research
Importance to the field	Topics of particular timely relevance?	Topical relevance; importance of the subject
Interest to *JMMR* readership	What communities of people (both within and beyond anthropology) are likely to be engaged by this essay?	

- The criteria among the three qualitative research journals show distinctive differences.
  - *Cultural Anthropology* highlights the degree of rich descriptions and innovation.
  - The *Journal of Ethnographic and Qualitative Research* highlights the fundamental steps of conducting research.
  - *International Sociology* highlights ways in which argument is made.
- *JMMR* highlights the fit of research questions to design.
- Criteria such as researcher credentials and ethics are less explicit than in the past.

The human subject criterion noted in the first column of Table 4.1 refers to specific explanations pertaining to either the power relationship between the researcher and the researched or the validity in the methods section, whereas contemporary research journals seek out information on institutional review boards as a required condition. That is, currently, when authors submit manuscripts or proposals, they are initially asked if their research fulfills a requirement of human subject review. Therefore, this criterion is less likely to be included in current review guidelines.

Conclusion

In this chapter, I examined three aspects of the evaluation of qualitative research, all of which have to do with natural, political, and epistemological changes in the 21st century. First, this chapter observed a change in the set of evaluative criteria by the same scholars over time. That is, can one change a set of evaluative criteria formulated in the past in an effort to better address what is now believed to be best? Of course one can. As time passes, it is reasonable that one might have to adjust existing principles and practices to better fit emerging needs. Nonetheless, caution may be needed. To a large extent, evaluation is partially personal, social, and political in nature. When such a change is made, it is important to explain why. Perhaps the more one knows about such changes and modifications from various scholars and researchers, the better one can make sense of the complex evaluation of qualitative research.

Second, qualitative research faces a new challenge and attack from those who define research very narrowly. The notion of scientific research that has been adopted by many national organizations is only convergent with endorsing two traditional research methods—experimental and correlational designs. It is time to listen to Lee Cronbach (1957), who invented one of the most famous reliability coefficients in statistics, Cronbach's alpha. His concern with these two narrowly practiced designs is still valid. He noted, "Correlational psychology studies only variance among organisms; experimental psychology studies only variance among treatments. A united discipline will study both of these, but it will also be concerned with the otherwise neglected interactions between organismic and treatment variables" (p. 671). Cronbach implies that great caution is needed to generalize a finding from samples to the target population mainly because of history and the idiosyncratic nature of human beings. As such, experimental designs and correlation research should not be considered appropriate only for complex contexts such as classrooms, where many compounding variables exist. It is suggested that the qualitative research community continue to create an open dialogue with positivists and policymakers to share not only what qualitative research is but also how it is evaluated. Again, we qualitative researchers may have to seriously prepare to answer a difficult question: Can qualitative researchers answer policymakers' "what works" question? (Donmoyer, 2012).

Last, it is time that we qualitative researchers learn more about what mixed methods researchers have done during the past few years. It is not meaningful to bring the binary question, "Are they our ally or enemy?" to the table. A continuing dialogue with these hard-working scholars is necessary. The bottom line is that whether mixed methods research is seen as a myth or something that is unavoidable at this time in this era, it is creeping into our everyday lives. This trend is something we cannot avoid and thus realistically must accept. Nonetheless, we qualitative researchers should not be tolerant if our century-long, complex, profound, intellectual knowledge base is treated as trivial facts or techniques from mixed methods researchers' quick and fast "what works" menu.

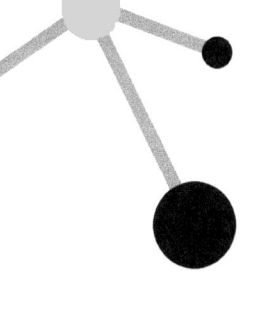

5

GETTING OUT OF THE FIELD

Criteria in the 21st century are not one-dimensional.

—Lichtman (2006, p. 197)

THIS BOOK explores an exciting, creative, but difficult topic that has often been mentioned but that has seldom been fully discussed and synthesized in the academic research community: how to conceptually understand and practically evaluate the quality of qualitative research. As a matter of fact, the word "evaluation" can cause one to feel uneasy. It is not a simple task to accomplish. Who evaluates what? How? From which/whose perspective? More important, by which/whose/what criteria? To make things more complicated, Why evaluate? There are pioneers or giants in the qualitative research community who have demonstrated ideas and methods through their own intellectual foundations, such as paradigm talks, philosophical discourses, theoretical constructs, and practical suggestions. The languages that these leading scholars have used vary, depending on the aspect of understanding and assessing the quality of qualitative research.

Despite the fact that there are few scholarly pieces regarding qualitative research, the depth and creativity that these pioneering researchers have demonstrated are profound, and the extent to which they cover not only the broad quality of qualitative research but also most of the specific qualities expected by many different kinds of qualitative research is incredible. In essence, this book has attempted to go beyond these intellectual foods available today by specifically focusing on what is needed to create the "evaluation of qualitative research 2.0" in the future.

In Chapter 1, the scope of this book was modestly determined as I addressed where this field of evaluating qualitative research is located in reference to languages or keywords that have existed since 1985 when the book *Naturalistic Inquiry* (Lincoln & Guba, 1985) was published.

In Chapter 2, five categories were identified as a typology of the evaluation of qualitative research, and I believe that this typology is a creative synthesis of existing philosophical, theoretical, and practical literature. This typology may not be mutually exclusive, but it comprehensively covers substantial contents of the literature in terms of different rationales necessary for answering the "why" question. In effect, these different rationales for the evaluation of qualitative research suggest different approaches on how to evaluate the different qualities present in different kinds of qualitative research. A representative example of evaluative form was introduced in each category. Last, this chapter introduced a holistic view of these different approaches of evaluating qualitative research, one that belongs to the author's scholarly lens to see different ideas connected. Qualitative research is not a unified field of study. Differences in kind have always existed, been recognized, and accepted in the qualitative research community. The hexagonal approach to the evaluation of qualitative research should be regarded as a broad, synthesized, creative way to make better sense of the differences in qualitative research.

Chapter 3 provided the reader with a number of different review examples on how to evaluate different qualities in different kinds of qualitative research. These practical examples were available in both scholarly writings and actual research journals. As expected, common criteria were used across different kinds of qualitative research, whereas particular criteria were used for specific types of qualitative research. Some had four to six genetic criteria. Others had a number of procedural criteria. Still others had a mix of both genetic and procedural criteria. Whereas some had very simple forms, others had complex forms. In my analysis of all these review criteria, I found none of them to be the same; all had possible strengths and weaknesses. Note, however, that whether or not qualitative research journals have an official form for a review guide depends primarily on their intellectual traditions and methodological choices. It is likely not the case that using such specific assessment tools results in the reviewer producing a better review. By examining 18 qualitative research journals' evaluation review guides, I constructed an analysis table of the most frequently used evaluation criteria.

Chapter 4 dealt with the socially constructed nature of evaluation criteria, politics of evidence, and the evaluation of mixed methods research. All of these topics revealed some confusion, some intensified pressure on the qualitative research community, and some strange feelings regarding qualitative methodologists. To simplify, what/which criteria should be included and excluded depends on, to a larger sense, personal, professional, and political choices. Personal growth, the social world, and political climates are constantly changing.

I close this book with two quotations, an important finding from my inquiry, and an imaginative wishful story. The first quotation is what I call "Lost, but not really lost" from Morse (2011), editor of *Qualitative Health Journal*:

What do you do when you find that *none* of your data appear relevant to, or answer, your research question? You have worked hard at gathering data, have got into analysis by coding and forming themes or categories, but when you really look at these data, none seem to fit your research question. It is not really that you have no data at all; the problem is you have no pertinent data that address your question. You did everything right. You began your study with an armchair walkthrough, considered the literature, negotiated with the gatekeepers, took your time in getting in so that trusting relationships could be established with participants, yet your project fell apart. No one said it would be easy, yet no one said it was impossible. When such disasters happen, I console by saying, "All the easy topics have been taken. Only the hard, really significant ones are left." (p. 1163, emphasis in original)

The second quotation concerns self-criticality in the development and evaluation of qualitative research (Tracy, 2010):

> In demonstrating methodological excellence, we need to take care of ourselves in the process of taking care of others. The most successful researchers are willingly self-critical, viewing their own actions through the eyes of others while also maintaining resilience and energy through acute sensitivity to their own well-being. (p. 849)

Table 5.1 presents important findings of my inquiry.

Now, let me get out of the field. We qualitative researchers live with a feeling of uncertainty before, during, and after fieldwork. During this ongoing feeling of uncertainty, we are trained to be self-critical in making the research we conduct be both convergent and divergent. At some point, we come to realize that the key to success in our research is dependent on the researcher participant. We do our best in hopes that we address everything we can to produce the best quality research. Later, the destiny of our paper is dependent on the journal editors and reviewers. I am sure they must have felt the same about qualitative research when they were beginning researchers back then. As indicated in Table 5.1, *trust* between a journal editor and a reviewer is seen as effective. By the same token, all these key criteria that a reviewer is asked to keep in

Table 5.1

Four Rationales for Non-Use of Specific Review Guides and Seven Most Commonly Used Criteria Across Select Qualitative Review Guides

Four Rationales	Seven Most Commonly Used Criteria
Trust: Reviewers do their job.	Importance to the field
Freedom: Reviewers do a better job without any restrictions.	Qualities
	Writing
The nature of qualitative research: Qualitative research is art.	Data analysis
	Theoretical framework
It works: Editors can still receive good-quality reviews.	Participant
	Impact/readership

mind in the review process appear to work in practice. We qualitative researchers may agree with the fact that our senior researchers produced quality research products in the past without knowing these assessment tools.

Are junior qualitative researchers currently producing quality research products with and without these assessment tools? Of course they are. As such, these assessment tools must have served as a function of evaluation from the third party. At the same time, however, these assessment tools must have served as a dialogical space in which an author of a paper and a reviewer imaginatively sit together to have a cup of coffee and talk about the most important qualities. The real fundamental question is, "Did this coffee break between the author of the paper and the reviewer begin from the very moment when submitting her/his institutional review board proposal?" Furthermore, "Did this coffee break occur when a junior qualitative researcher turned in his/her first fieldwork-related term paper in the introductory to qualitative research?" I hope the answers are "yes" and "yes."

I thank the readers of this book for accepting my invitation to this new field of study. Together, we qualitative researchers now can say, "Fortunately, there are commonly agreed, bold standards for evaluating the goodness of qualitative research in the academic research community. These standards are a part of what is generally called 'scientific research.'" I hope my wish can come true now (or in the near future).

Additional Reading

Qualitative Research

The following is a list of additional reading that the reader may find useful for broadening a general scope of qualitative research. Included are journal articles and books that deal with a variety of topics, including interviews, positionality, multicultural education, design, arts-based research, Internet-mediated research, ethics, reflexivity, social fiction, post-structuralism, postmodernism, dictionary, auto- and duo-ethnography, analysis, computer-assisted data analysis, writing, and so on.

Bevan, M. (2014). A method of phenomenological interviewing. *Qualitative Health Research*, 24(1), 136–144.

Bourke, B. (2014). Positionality: Reflecting on the research process. *The Qualitative Report, 19* (How to Article 18), 1–9. Retrieved from http://www.nova.edu/ssss/QR/QR19/bourke18.pdf

Brinkmann, S., & Kvale, S. (2015). *InterViews: Learning the craft of qualitative research interviewing* (3rd ed.). Thousand Oaks, CA: Sage.

Deakin, H., & Wakefield, K. (2013). Skype interviewing: Reflections of two PhD researchers. *Journal of Qualitative Research, 14*(5), 603–616.

Dixon, A. (2014). *Researching race in education: Policy, practice and qualitative research.* Charlotte, NC: Information Age Publishing.

Flyybjerg, B. (2006). Five misunderstandings about case-study research. *Qualitative Inquiry, 12*(2), 219–245.

Given, L. (2015). *100 questions (and answers) about qualitative research.* Thousand Oaks, CA: Sage.

Guillemin, M., & Gillam, L. (2004). Ethics, reflexivity, and "ethically important moments" in research. *Qualitative Inquiry, 10*(2), 261–280.

Hewson, C. (2014). Qualitative approaches in Internet-mediated research: Opportunities, issues, possibilities. In P. Leavy (Ed.), *The Oxford handbook of qualitative research* (pp. 423–451). New York, NY: Oxford University Press.

Holman Jones, S., Adams, T., & Ellis, C. (Eds.). (2013). *Handbook of autoethnography.* Walnut Creek, CA: Left Coast Press.

Hsieh, H., & Shannon, S. (2005). Three approaches to qualitative content analysis. *Qualitative Health Research, 15*(9), 1277–1288.

Jagodzinski, J., & Wallin, J. (2013). *Arts-based research: A critique and a proposal.* Rotterdam, the Netherlands: Sense Publishers.

Koro-Ljungberg, M. (2015). *Reconceptualizing qualitative research: Methodologies without methodology.* Thousand Oaks, CA: Sage.

Leavy, P. (2015). *Methods meets art: Arts-based research practice* (2nd ed.). New York, NY: Guilford Press.

Leavy, P. (2017). *Research design: Quantitative, qualitative, mixed methods, arts-based, and community-based participatory research approaches.* New York, NY: Guilford Press.

Madison, D. S. (2005). *Critical ethnography: Method, ethics, and performance.* Thousand Oaks, CA: Sage.

Marshall, C., & Rossman, G. (2015). *Designing qualitative research* (6th ed.). Thousand Oaks, CA: Sage.

Maxwell, J. (2010). Using numbers in qualitative research. *Qualitative Inquiry, 16*(6), 475–482.

Norris, J., Sawyer, R., & Lund, D. (Eds.). (2012). *Duoethnography: Dialogical methods for social, health, and educational research.* Walnut Creek, CA: Left Coast Press.

Rolling, J. H., Jr. (2013). *Arts-based research primer.* New York, NY: Lang.

Saldana, J. (2015). *Thinking qualitatively: Methods of mind.* Thousand Oaks, CA: Sage.

Silver, C., & Lewins, A. (2014). Computer-assisted analysis of qualitative research. In P. Leavy (Ed.), *The Oxford handbook of qualitative research* (pp. 606–638). New York, NY: Oxford University Press.

St. Pierre, E., & Jackson, A. (2014). Qualitative data analysis after coding. *Qualitative Inquiry, 20*(6), 715–719.

Sturges, J., & Hanrahan, K. (2004). Comparing telephone and face-to-face qualitative interviewing: A research note. *Journal of Qualitative Research, 4*(1), 107–118.

Mixed Methods Research

The following is a list of additional reading that the reader may find useful for broadening a general scope of mixed methods research. Included are articles and books that deal with a variety of topics, such as paradigm, design, sampling, analysis, triangulation, and so on.

Bergman, M. E. (Ed.). (2008). *Advances in mixed methods research.* Thousand Oaks, CA: Sage.

Burke, R. J., & Onwuegbuzie, A. (2004). Mixed methods research: A research paradigm whose time has come. *Educational Researcher, 33*(7), 14–26.

Creswell, J., & Clark, V. (2010). *Designing and conducting mixed methods research* (2nd ed.). Thousand Oaks, CA: Sage.

Curry, L., & Nunez-Smith, M. (2015). *Mixed methods in health sciences research: A practical primer.* Thousand Oaks, CA: Sage.

Dillman, D., Smyth, J., & Christian, L. (2014). *Internet, phone, mail, and mixed-mode surveys: The tailored design method* (4th ed.). Hoboken, NJ: Wiley.

Garner, J. (2015). Different ways to disagree: A study of organizational dissent to explore connections between mixed methods research and engaged scholarship. *Journal of Mixed Methods Research, 9*(2), 178–195.

Greene, J. (2007). *Mixed methods in social inquiry.* San Francisco, CA: Jossey-Bass.

Harrits, G. S. (2011). More than method? A discussion of paradigm differences within mixed methods research. *Journal of Mixed Methods Research, 5*(2), 150–166.

Howe, K. (2012). Mixed methods, triangulation, and causal explanation. *Journal of Mixed Methods Research, 6*(2), 89–96.

Mayoh, J., & Onwuegbuzie, A. (2015). Toward a conceptualization of mixed methods phenomenological research, *Journal of Mixed Methods Research, 9*(1), 91–107.

Mertens, D., & Hesse-Biber, S. (2012). Triangulation and mixed methods research: Provocative positions. *Journal of Mixed Methods Research, 6*(2), 75–79.

Morgan, D. (2007). Paradigms lost and pragmatism regained: Methodological implications of combining qualitative and quantitative methods. *Journal of Mixed Methods Research, 1*(1), 48–76.

Onwuegbuzie, J. (2003). A framework for analyzing data in mixed methods research. In A. Tashakkori & C. Teddlie (Eds.), *Handbook of mixed methods research* (pp. 351–383). Thousand Oaks, CA: Sage.

Tashakkori, A., & Creswell, J. (2007). The new era of mixed method research. *Journal of Mixed Methods Research, 1*(1), 3–7.

Tashakkori, A., & Teddlie, C. (Eds.). (2003). *Handbook of mixed methods research.* Thousand Oaks, CA: Sage.

Tashakkori, A., & Teddlie, C. (Eds.). (2010). *The Sage handbook of mixed methods in social and behavioral research* (2nd ed.). Thousand Oaks, CA: Sage.

Teddlie, C., & Tashakkori, A. (2009). *Foundations of mixed methods research: Integrating quantitative and qualitative approaches in the social and behavioral sciences.* Thousand Oaks, CA: Sage.

Teddlie, C., & Yu, F. (2007). Mixed methods sampling: A typology with examples. *Journal of Mixed Methods Research, 1*(1), 77–100.

Useful Websites for Qualitative Research

The following is a list of websites that the reader may find useful for broadening a general scope of qualitative research.

- QualPage, "Resources for Qualitative Research" (http://www. qualitativeresearch.uga.edu/QualPage/index.html): This website includes a wide range of resources, such as the following: Disciplines & Philosophical Foundations, Journals & Publishers, Theses & Papers, Proceedings, Methods, Multimedia & QDA, Organizations & Interest Groups, Other Websites, and Teaching Qualitative Research.
- Qualitative Research Guidelines Project, "Using Qualitative Methods in Healthcare Research" (http://www.qualres.org): The Robert Wood Johnson Foundation has sponsored the Qualitative Research Guidelines Project to develop a website that is useful for people developing, evaluating, and engaging in qualitative research projects in health care settings. Click on the individual Project Links for more information.
- *TQR (The Qualitative Research Report)* a weekly online journal dedicated to qualitative research (http://tqr.nova.edu): Click the Resources tab for a comprehensive list of qualitative research websites, all qualitative research journals, teaching and learning resources, and more.
- The Creativity Post: Quality Content on Creativity, Innovation, and Imagination (http://www.creativitypost.com): The Creativity Post is a nonprofit web platform committed to sharing the very best content on creativity, in all of its forms—from scientific discovery to philosophical debate, from entrepreneurial ventures to educational reform, from artistic expression to technological innovation—in short, all the varieties of the human experience that creativity brings to life.
- AQR, The Association for Qualitative Research: The Hub of Qualitative Thinking (http://www.aqr.org.uk): This UK website includes excellent resources, such as Glossary of Terms, Recommended Reading,

Professional Guidelines and FAQs, and Useful Contacts & Country Guides. It also has In Brief and In Depth, both of which deal with newly emerging issues, commentary articles, and future directions.

- The Grounded Theory Institute: The Official Site of Dr. Barney Glaser and Classic Grounded Theory (http://www.groundedtheory.org): This website provides extensive information about grounded theory, in addition to ongoing seminars, related books, online forum, and so on.
- QRCA: Qualitative Research Consultants Association (http://qrca.site-ym.com): QRCA is a not-for-profit association of consultants involved in the design and implementation of qualitative research—focus groups, in-depth interviews, in-context and observational research, and more. In particular, this website has resources for marketers/market researchers and for qualitative research practitioners.
- Electronic Resources for Research Methods (http://informationr.net/rm): This website has a comprehensive list of topics on both qualitative and quantitative research methods. There are many useful resources related to qualitative research.
- Qualitative Research in Information Systems (http://www.qual.auckland.ac.nz): This site aims to provide qualitative researchers—and those wanting to know how to do qualitative research—with useful information on the conduct, evaluation, and publication of qualitative research.
- Centre for Qualitative Research by Bournemouth University (https://research.bournemouth.ac.uk/centre/centre-for-qualitative-research): The reader will find very informative resources on qualitative research in areas of Humanising Health and Social Care, Novel and Innovative Research Methodologies, and Performative Social Science.
- Arts-Based Research Studio (http://arts-basedresearchstudio.ning.com/page/about): The Arts-Based Research Studio, at the University of Alberta, is an initiative started by Dr. Diane Conrad. It is a place where researchers from diverse faculties partake in conversation, presentation, and performance on a breadth of topics. The principal points around which researchers gather, talk, and invite presentations are, although not exclusively, art, aesthetics, and civic consciousness. The space itself is fully accessible and inclusive and is located in the Education Centre on the University of Alberta campus.
- METHODS—Qualitative (http://gsociology.icaap.org/methods/qual.htm): This page lists free resources for social research methods. The focus is on how to do social research: surveys, focus groups, sampling, interviews, and other methods.

REFERENCES

Aguinaldo, J. P. (2004). Rethinking validity in qualitative research from a social constructionist perspective: From "Is this valid research?" to "What is this research valid for?" *The Qualitative Report, 9*(1), 127–136. Retrieved from http://nsuworks.nova.edu/cgi/viewcontent.cgi?article=1941&context=tqr

Ambert, A., Adler, P., Adler, P., & Detzner, D. (1995). Understanding and evaluating qualitative research. *Journal of Marriage and Family, 57*(4), 879–893.

American Educational Research Association. (2006). Standards for reporting on empirical social science research in AERA publications. *Educational Researcher, 35*(6), 33–40.

Barone, T., & Eisner, E. (2012). *Arts based research.* Thousand Oaks, CA: Sage.

Burns, N. (1989). Standards for qualitative research. *Nursing Science Quarterly, 2*(1), 44–52.

Chenail, R. J., Cooper, R., Patron, L.,& TQR Associates. (2011). *The Qualitative Report (TQR) rubric.* Fort Lauderdale, FL: TQR Community. Retrieved from http://www.nova.edu/ssss/QR/TQR_Rubric_2011.pdf

Cho, J., & Trent, A. (2006). Validity in qualitative research revisited. *Journal of Qualitative Research, 6*(3), 319–340.

Cho, J., & Trent, A. (2009). Validity criteria for performance-related qualitative work: Toward a reflexive, evaluative, and co-constructive framework for performance in/as qualitative inquiry. *Qualitative Inquiry, 15*(6), 1013–1041.

Clifford, J. (1986). Introduction: Partial truths. In J. Clifford & G. Marcus (Eds.), *Writing culture: The poetics and politics of ethnography* (pp. 1–26). Berkeley, CA: University of California Press.

Cobb, A., & Hagemaster, J. (1987). Ten criteria for evaluating qualitative research proposals. *Journal of Nursing Education, 26*(4), 138–143.

Corbin, J., & Strauss, A. (2008). *Basics of qualitative research* (3rd ed.). Thousand Oaks, CA: Sage.

Creswell, J. (2008). *Educational research: Planning, conducting, and evaluating quantitative and qualitative research* (3rd ed.). Boston, MA: Pearson.

Creswell, J. (2012). *Qualitative inquiry and research design: Choosing among five approaches* (3rd ed.). Thousand Oaks, CA: Sage.

Creswell, J., & Clark, P. (2007). *Designing and conducting mixed methods research.* Thousand Oaks, CA: Sage.

Cronbach, L. (1957). The two disciplines of scientific psychology. *American Psychologist, 2*(11), 671–684.

Denzin, N. (2009). The elephant in the living room: Or extending the conversation about the politics of evidence. *Qualitative Inquiry, 9*(2), 139–160.

Denzin, N. (2012). Triangulation 2.0. *Journal of Mixed Methods Research, 6*(2), 80–88.

Denzin, N., & Giardina, M. (2009). Introduction. In N. Denzin & M. Giardian (Eds.), *Qualitative inquiry and social justice* (pp. 11–50). Walnut Creek, CA: Left Coast Press.

Denzin, N., & Lincoln, Y. (Eds.). (1994). *The handbook of qualitative research.* Thousand Oaks, CA: Sage.

Denzin, N., & Lincoln, Y. (Eds.). (2000). *The handbook of qualitative research* (2nd ed.). Thousand Oaks, CA: Sage.

Denzin, N., & Lincoln, Y. (Eds.). (2005). *The Sage handbook of qualitative research* (3rd ed.). Thousand Oaks, CA: Sage.

Denzin, N., & Lincoln, Y. (Eds.). (2011). *The Sage handbook of qualitative research* (4th ed.). Thousand Oaks, CA: Sage.

Dixon, A., & Dodo Seriki, V. (2013). Positional and identity-based theories of research. In A. Trainor & E. Graue (Eds.), *Reviewing qualitative research in the social sciences* (pp. 212–215). New York, NY: Routledge.

Donmoyer, R. (2012). Can qualitative researchers answers policy-makers' simple "what works" question? *Qualitative Inquiry, 18*(8), 662–673.

Duncan, S., & Harrop, A. (2006). A user perspective on research quality. *International Journal of Social Research Methodology, 9*(2), 159–174.

Elliott, R., Fischer, C., & Rennie, D. (1999). Evolving guidelines for publication of qualitative research studies in psychology and related fields. *British Journal of Clinical Psychology, 38*(3), 215–299.

Forchuk, C., & Roberts, J. (1993). How to critique qualitative research articles. *Canadian Journal of Nursing Research, 25*(4), 47–56.

Geertz, C. (1998). Deep hanging out. *New York Review of Books, 45*(16), 69–72.

Gómez, C. (2009). Assessing the quality of qualitative health research: Criteria, process and writing. *Forum: Qualitative Social Research, 10*(2), Art. 17. Retrieved from http://nbn-resolving.de/urn:nbn:de:0114-fqs0902178

Greene, J. (2000). Understanding social programs through evaluation. In N. Denzin & Y. Lincoln (Eds.), *The handbook of qualitative research* (2nd ed., pp. 981–999). Thousand Oaks, CA: Sage.

Greenhalgh, T. (1997). Assessing the methodological quality of published papers. *BMJ, 315*(7103), 305–308.

Guba, E. (Ed.). (1990). *The paradigm dialog.* Newbury Park, CA: Sage.

Guba, E., & Lincoln, Y. (1989). *Fourth generation evaluation.* Newbury Park, CA: Sage.

Guba, E., & Lincoln, Y. (1994). Competing paradigms in qualitative research. In N. Denzin & Y. Lincoln (Eds.), *The handbook of qualitative research* (pp. 105–117). Thousand Oaks, CA: Sage.

Guba, E., & Lincoln, Y. (2000). Paradigmatic controversies, contradictions, and emerging confluences. In N. Denzin & Y. Lincoln (Eds.), *The handbook of qualitative research* (2nd ed., pp. 163–188). Thousand Oaks, CA: Sage.

Guba, E., & Lincoln, Y. (2005). Paradigmatic controversies, contradictions, and emerging confluences. In N. Denzin & Y. Lincoln (Eds.), *The Sage handbook of qualitative research* (3rd ed., pp. 191–216). Thousand Oaks, CA: Sage.

Guillemin, N., & Gillam, L. (2004). Ethics, reflexivity, and "ethically important moments" in research. *Qualitative Inquiry, 10*(2), 261–280.

Hamera, J. (2006). Introduction: Opening opening acts. In J. Hamera (Ed.), *Opening acts: Performance in/as communication and cultural studies* (pp. 1–10). Thousand Oaks, CA: Sage.

Hamera, J., & Conquergood, D. (2006). Performance and politics: Themes and arguments. In D. S. Madison & J. Hamera (Eds.), *The Sage handbook of performance studies* (pp. 419–425). Thousand Oaks, CA: Sage.

Hammersley, M. (2008). Troubles with triangulation. In M. M. Bergman (Ed.), *Advances in mixed methods research* (pp. 22–36). Los Angeles, CA: Sage.

Hammersley, M., & Atkinson, P. (1995). *Ethnography: Principles in practice* (2nd ed.). London, UK: Routledge.

Hancock, G., & Mueller, R. (Eds.). (2010). *The reviewer's guide to quantitative methods in the social sciences.* New York, NY: Taylor & Francis.

Heyvaert, M., Hannes, K., Maes, B., & Onghena, P. (2013). Critical appraisal of mixed methods studies. *Journal of Mixed Methods Research, 7*(4), 302–327.

Inui, T., & Frankel, R. (1991). Evaluating the quality of qualitative research. *Journal of General Internal Medicine, 6,* 485–486.

Janesick, V. (2013). Oral history, life history, and biography. In A. Trainor & E. Graue (Eds.), *Reviewing qualitative research in the social sciences* (pp. 154–161). New York, NY: Routledge.

Lather, P. (1986). Issues of validity in openly ideological research: Between a rock and a soft place. *Interchange, 17*(4), 63–84.

Lather, P. (1993). Fertile obsession: Validity after poststructuralism. *The Sociological Quarterly, 34*(4), 673–693.

Lather, P. (2007). *Getting lost: Feminist efforts towards a double(d) science.* New York, NY: State University of New York Press.

Leavy, P. (Ed.). (2014). *The Oxford handbook of qualitative research.* New York, NY: Oxford University Press.

Leech, N., Dellinger, A., Brannagan, K., & Tanaka, H. (2010). Evaluating mixed research studies: A mixed methods approach. *Journal of Mixed Methods Research, 4*(1), 17–31.

Lichtman, M. (2006). *Qualitative research in education: A user's guide.* Thousand Oaks, CA: Sage.

Lichtman, M. (2014). *Qualitative research for the social sciences.* Thousand Oaks, CA: Sage.

Lincoln, Y., & Guba, G. (1985). *Naturalistic inquiry.* Newbury Park, CA: Sage.

Lincoln, Y., Lynham, S., & Guba, E. (2011). Paradigmatic controversies, contradictions, and emerging confluences, revisited. In N. Denzin & Y. Lincoln (Eds.), *The Sage handbook of qualitative research* (4th ed., pp. 97–128). Thousand Oaks, CA: Sage.

Madrid, S. (2007). *Emotional themes in preschool children's play narratives.* Unpublished doctoral dissertation, The Ohio State University, Columbus, OH.

Marshall, C. (1990). Goodness criteria: Are they objective or judgment calls? In E. Guba & Y. Lincoln (Eds.), *The paradigm dialogue* (pp. 188–197). Newbury Park, CA: Sage.

Maxwell, J. (1992). Understanding and validity in qualitative research. *Harvard Educational Review, 62,* 279–299.

Maxwell, J. (1996). *Qualitative research design: An interpretive approach.* Thousand Oaks, CA: Sage.

Mertens, D. (2013). Mixed methods. In A. Trainor & E. Graue (Eds.), *Reviewing qualitative research in the social sciences* (pp. 141–147). New York, NY: Routledge.

Miles, M., & Huberman, M. *(1994). Qualitative data analysis: A sourcebook of new methods.* Beverly Hills, CA: Sage.

Morse, J. (1991). Evaluating qualitative research. *Qualitative Health Research, 1*(3), 283–286.

Morse, J. (2011). The case of the missing data. *Qualitative Health Research, 21*(9), 1163–1164.

Patton, M. (2002). *Qualitative research and evaluation methods* (3rd ed.). Thousand Oaks, CA: Sage.

Prendergast, M., & Belliveau, G. (2013). Poetics and performance. In A. Trainor & E. Graue (Eds.), *Reviewing qualitative research in the social sciences* (pp. 201–204). New York, NY: Routledge.

Richardson, L. (2000). Writing: A method of inquiry. In N. Denzin & Y. Lincoln (Eds.), *The handbook of qualitative research* (2nd ed., pp. 923–948). Thousand Oaks, CA: Sage.

Richardson, L., & St. Pierre, E. (2005). Writing: A method of inquiry. In N. Denzin & Y. Lincoln (Eds.), *The Sage handbook of qualitative research* (3rd ed., pp. 959–978). Thousand Oaks, CA: Sage.

Riessman, C. (2008). *Narrative methods for the human sciences.* Thousand Oaks, CA: Sage.

Sale, J., & Brazil, K. (2004). A strategy to identify critical appraisal criteria for primary mixed-methods studies. *Quality & Quantity, 38,* 351–365.

Scheurich, J. (1996). The masks of validity: A deconstructive investigation. *International Journal of Qualitative Studies in Education, 9*(1), 49–60.

Schwandt, T. (2002). *Evaluation practice reconsidered.* New York, NY: Lang.

Seale, C. (1999). *The quality of qualitative research.* London, UK: Sage.

Seale, C. (2002). Qualitative issues in qualitative inquiry. *Qualitative Social Work, 1*(1), 97–110.

Smith, J. (1990). Alternative research paradigms and the problem of criteria. In E. Guba (Ed.), *The paradigm dialog* (pp. 167–187). Newbury Park, CA: Sage.

Stiles, W. (1999). Evaluating qualitative research. *Evidence-Based Mental Health*, *2*(4), 99–101.

Stucky, N., & Wimmer, C. (Eds.). (2002). *Teaching performance studies*. Carbondale, IL: Southern Illinois University Press.

Tashakkori, A., & Teddlie, C. (2008). Quality of inferences in mixed methods research: Calling for an integrative framework. In M. M. Bergman (Ed.), *Advances in mixed methods research* (pp. 101–119). Los Angeles, CA: Sage.

Thomas, E., & Magilvy, J. (2011). Qualitative rigor or research validity in qualitative research. *Journal of Specialists in Pediatric Nursing*, *16*, 151–155.

Tong, A., Sainsbury, P., & Craig, J. (2007). Consolidated Criteria for Reporting Qualitative Research (COREQ): A 32-item checklist for interviews and focus groups. *International Journal of Qualitative Health Care*, *19*(6), 349–357.

Tracy, S. (2010). Qualitative quality: Eight "big-tent" criteria for excellent qualitative research. *Qualitative Inquiry*, *16*(10), 837–851.

Trainor, A., & Graue, E. (Eds.). (2013). *Reviewing qualitative research in the social sciences*. New York, NY: Routledge.

Watson, C. (2009). Picturing validity: Autoethnography and the representation of self? *Qualitative Inquiry*, *15*(3), 526–544.

ABOUT THE AUTHOR

Jeasik Cho is a professor of Educational Studies Department in the College of Education at the University of Wyoming. He is awarded the 2016–18 Everett D. and Elizabeth M. Lantz Outstanding Professorship. He received his doctorate at The Ohio State University in 2000 and had a post-doc experience with Dr. Robert Donmoyer at the University of San Diego in 2001. He teaches undergraduate and graduate courses: An Introduction to Qualitative Research, Advanced Qualitative Research Methods, Educational Assessment, and Classroom Assessment for Teaching and Learning. His scholarly work in qualitative research, curriculum theory, performance assessment, and multicultural education/critical race theory appears in *Qualitative Research Journal, Qualitative Inquiry, QSE: International Journal of Qualitative Studies in Education, The Qualitative Report, TABOO: The Journal of Culture and Education, Multicultural Educational Review, The Oxford Handbook of Qualitative Research, Encyclopedia of Curriculum Studies, Curriculum and Assessment for Pre-Service Teachers, Action Research for Educational Improvement*, and so on.

INDEX